HOW TO MAKE
SILVER CHARMS
FROM METAL CLAY

HOW TO MAKE SILVER CHARMS FROM METAL CLAY

Sue Heaser

A QUARTO BOOK

Copyright © 2013 Quarto Inc.

This edition for North America and
the Philippines first published in 2013
by Barron's Educational Series, Inc.

All inquiries should be addressed to:
Barron's Educational Series, Inc.
250 Wireless Boulevard
Hauppauge, NY 11788
www.barronseduc.com

ISBN: 978-1-4380-0262-0
Library of Congress Control Number:
2013939230

Conceived, designed, and produced by
Quarto Publishing plc
The Old Brewery
6 Blundell Street
London N7 9BH

QUA: MCSC

Editor: Michelle Pickering
Art director: Caroline Guest
Designer: Tanya Goldsmith
Illustrator: Kuo Kang Chen
Photographer: Phil Wilkins
Indexer: Helen Snaith
Creative director: Moira Clinch
Publisher: Paul Carslake

Color separation by Modern Age
Repro House Ltd., Hong Kong
Printed by 1010 Printing
International Ltd., China

9 8 7 6 5 4 3 2 1

Contents

Introduction

Charms have always held enchantment for me and even the word "charm" has a delightful ring to it. Charms are tiny ornaments that are made in a fascinating variety of shapes and designs. They are usually made in precious metals and can be worn as jewelry, kept as keepsakes and good luck talismans, incorporated into all kinds of handicrafts and artwork, or given as gifts and mementoes. Fashions come and go but charms have been popular for thousands of years, from the tiny golden charms of ancient Egypt to celebrity charms of today.

The advent of silver clays means that it is now possible to create your own silver charms at home without complicated equipment and, because they are so small, the cost of the materials is relatively small as well.

This book features 50 different projects, each with several variations. They range from traditional horseshoes, hearts, and padlocks to modern designs such as fashionable bead charms and quirky fish. Every project in the book uses no-kiln simple firing techniques, as well as a minimum of basic tools that are widely available and inexpensive.

My aim has been to design projects for all abilities, so whether you are a beginner or experienced in metal clay, I hope you will find plenty to delight you in these pages.

About this book

Here are a few guidelines to help you find your way around this book.

Choosing charms On pages 8–13 you will find some examples of finished charm bracelets, necklaces, earrings, and other items to inspire you with ideas for what kind of charm accessory you might like to make. You can then turn to the charm selector on pages 16–19, where you will find all 50 charm projects displayed together to help you choose which individual charms to make.

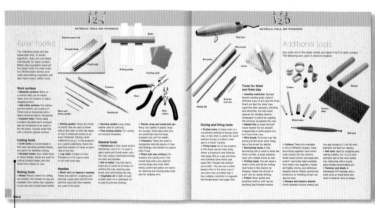

Basic toolkit The basic toolkit comprises the essential tools for working with silver clay and those that are used repeatedly when making charms. To avoid repetition, these tools are not listed individually for each project; refer to page 124 for the full list. Any additional tools required are listed in the relevant project, along with all of the materials.

Metal clay *Each project specifies the amount of silver clay required for each charm. Some charms require more clay to allow for rolling out and cutting shapes and these have the extra quantity given. After the charm is cut out, the excess clay can be saved for another project. Although silver clay is used to make all of the projects in this book, any other metal clay—such as gold, bronze, or copper—can be used instead. The only difference is in the firing, so you should refer to the manufacturer's instructions for that.*

Size of charms *Each project features an actual size photograph of a finished charm and an enlarged diagram with the charm's dimensions. These dimensions are of the piece as it is made, so that you can use them as a guide when making the charm. The finished charm will be slightly smaller because of shrinkage during firing. PMC3 charms will be about 12–15% smaller, while Art Clay Silver charms will be 8–9% smaller. You can make charms larger or smaller than given in the diagrams and instructions, but try to keep the proportions the same.*

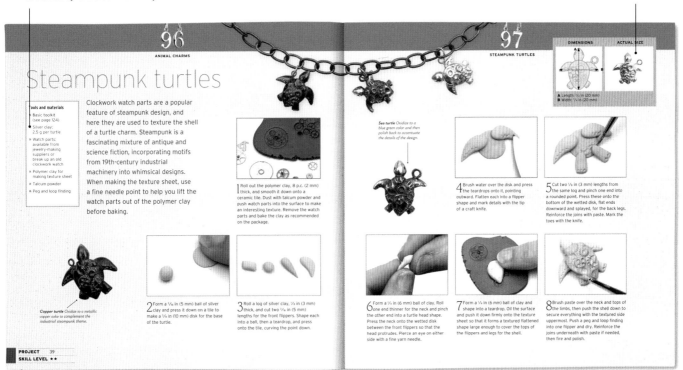

Star rating system *The star symbols at the bottom left-hand corner of each project indicate what skills you will need to make that particular charm.*
✳ = Requires only simple skills. Suitable for all abilities. Beginners should attempt these projects first to gain a little experience before moving on to two or three star projects.
✳✳ = A little more ability is needed than for one star.
✳✳✳ = These projects are more demanding or intricate to make. Try these after you have had some practice with silver clay.

Basic techniques *All of the projects are explained with step-by-step photographs and instructions, but at the back of the book (pages 126–141) you will find a summary of the core techniques of working with silver clay. Use this section as a refresher course if you need to brush up on basic skills.*

Measurements *These are given as imperial with metric equivalents, except for the thickness of clay sheets, where playing cards (p.c.) are used in place of imperial (see page 124 for explanation). Metal clay weight and drill bit and gemstone sizes are given in metric only, as this is how they are sold.*

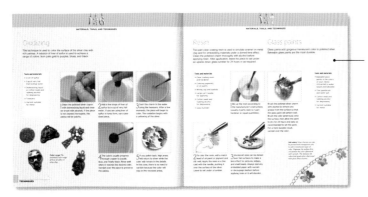

Springtime necklace
For a fresh and feminine look, combine multicolored flower and butterfly charms (pages 36 and 42) with bead dangles (page 141) on a large link necklace chain. Space the charms carefully to achieve an attractive hang.

Strawberry hoops
Luscious strawberry bead charms (page 112) are threaded onto large earring hoops with green and silver glass beads. To make the bead charms hang better on the hoops, use a darning needle to make smaller holes through the strawberries than you would make for a bracelet or necklace. Thread bead crimps on either side of the beads to hold everything in place.

Heart earrings
These graceful drop earrings are made with hearts but stars would look equally attractive. Attach two different heart charms (page 20) to short lengths of chain and then link the top of each chain to a loop and ball ear stud.

We ♥ charms

There are dozens of wonderful ways to wear and display charms, from gorgeous charm bracelets to embellishments for accessories and more unusual jewelry. The following pages will give you ideas to make the most of your charms.

A charm bracelet is the traditional way to wear charms, and many a little girl has been given a silver bracelet with a single charm for her birthday, to be added to over the years. Charms go naturally with celebrations, and a greeting card can contain a charm to be worn after the event. Charm parties can be held for a prospective bride, with every guest making the bride a charm for her wedding bracelet. Try hanging charms on a wire loop from champagne glasses for a special occasion, or attaching an angel charm to a gift for a new baby. A charm bracelet for a grandmother's special birthday with silhouette charms of all her grandchildren will become a precious heirloom.

Charms are not just for girls. Charms were traditionally given to soldiers going off to war by their loved ones as good luck tokens; and a lucky fish charm pinned to a fisherman's hat is sure to help his catch. Pet collars are often embellished with a charm and can be practical as well, engraved with a name or telephone number.

Be adventurous with charms—a charm dangling from an earring or pinned to a lapel adds detail and interest. Charms on small lengths of chain topped with a small clasp can be attached or removed with ease so that they can be swapped around according to mood or occasion. Charms can be clipped to a purse, worn on an anklet, dangled from a bikini, clipped to a shoe or zipper, or attached to a cellphone. Have fun with charms!

Star and bead charm bracelet
Three different star charms (page 22) are attached to small converter beads (page 118) for this sparkling bracelet. A mixture of gemstone beads (page 110) is interspersed between the stars.

Animal lover's bracelet
Three coils of bracelet memory wire are threaded with sections of blue rubber jewelry tubing. Between each section of tubing, two silver beads provide an anchorage point for an animal charm (pages 84–97).

Children's bracelet
Elasticized charm bracelets are a popular choice for children because they are so easy to put on and take off. They have jump rings already attached to points around the bracelet from which to display a colorful collection of children's charms (pages 48–59).

Fashion necklace
It is always fun to combine charms on a particular theme. A dress charm (page 78) combined with a dainty shoe (page 74) are perfect for a party girl necklace. Attach the charms with short lengths of chain to an ornamental ring at the front of a chain necklace. A dangle of pink and purple beads adds color.

Bookworm's key chain charm
Always popular as small gifts, a key chain is really special with a silver charm attached. A little book (page 64) complete with paper pages for tiny notes or telephone numbers makes an unusual and useful piece.

Letter cell phone charm
With so many identical cell phones, a charm dangle attached to your phone will make it stand out in the crowd. A simple chain carries a letter charm (page 102) along with a collection of berry colored beads.

Musical shawl pin
This shawl pin is made with 18-gauge (1 mm) sterling silver wire shaped on a wire jig and then hammered to flatten and strengthen it. Two music charms (page 62) are attached to the bottom loops for a music lover's shawl pin.

Purse charm
One of the simplest ways to display charms is using a silver-plated swivel clasp to attach charms to fashion accessories. A miniature purse charm (page 76) attached to the clasp is particularly suitable for clipping onto a bag or purse.

Projects

This chapter features 50 beautiful charm projects
organized into themed categories, from traditional
and nature charms to hobby and keepsake charms.
Lots of variations are provided to inspire you with
ideas for new charms and adaptations. In the following
four pages, you will find photographs of all the charms
together to help you make your selection.

Charm selector

Use this handy visual guide to help you select which charms to make, then turn to the relevant pages to begin. The charms are grouped into categories, and each design comes with several variations.

TRADITIONAL CHARMS

HEARTS 20

STARS 22

CROSSES 24

PADLOCKS 26

KEYS 28

LUCKY CLOVERS 30

HORSESHOES 32

COINS 34

CHARM SELECTOR

NATURE CHARMS	
	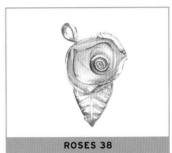
FLOWERS 36	ROSES 38

SHELLS 40	BUTTERFLIES 42

CHILDREN'S CHARMS

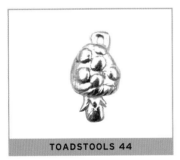			
TOADSTOOLS 44	SNOWFLAKES 46	FAIRIES 48	PUMPKIN COACHES 50

FLYING KITES 52	TEDDY BEARS 54	BABY RATTLES 56	DUCKLINGS 58

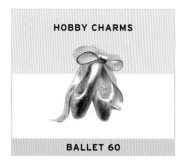

HOBBY CHARMS

BALLET 60

MUSIC 62

BOOKS 64

KNITTING 66

CARS 68

SAILING 70

TENNIS 72

FASHION CHARMS

HIGH-HEELED SHOES 74

PURSES 76

DRESSES 78

HATS 80

PARASOLS 82

ANIMAL CHARMS

DOGS 84

CATS 86

FISH 88

CHARM SELECTOR

BLUEBIRDS 90

HORSES 92

OWLS 94

STEAMPUNK TURTLES 96

KEEPSAKE CHARMS

PICTURE FRAMES 98

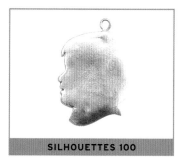

SILHOUETTES 100

LETTERS 102

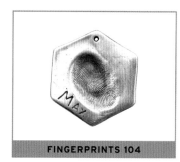

FINGERPRINTS 104

BIRTHDAY CAKES 106

CHAMPAGNE GLASSES 108

BEAD CHARMS

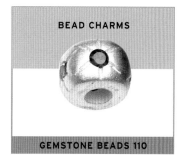

GEMSTONE BEADS 110

FRUIT 112

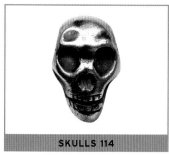

SKULLS 114

LITTLE HOUSES 116

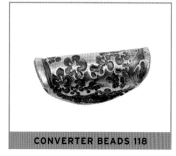

CONVERTER BEADS 118

Hearts

Heart-shaped charms have been favorites for centuries. They can symbolize love of many kinds, from romantic love to motherly love and the love between friends. This project uses the trick of cutting a heart shape through plastic wrap to give the edges a smoothly domed effect.

Tools and materials

- Basic toolkit (see page 124)
- Silver clay: 5 g for rolling out (each heart uses 1.5 g or less)
- Texture sheet
- Heart cutter: ½ in (13 mm) or smaller

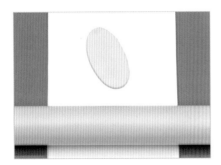

1 Roll out the clay on a non-stick surface using 6 p.c. (1.5 mm) rolling guides.

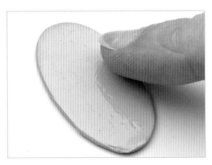

2 Lightly oil the top surface of the clay. Peel the clay off the work surface and place oiled side down on a texture sheet.

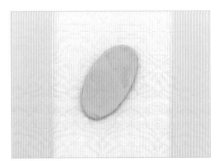

3 Place 4 p.c. (1 mm) rolling guides on either side of the clay on the texture sheet and roll again to texture the surface of the clay.

HEARTS

DIMENSIONS

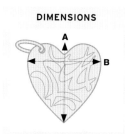

ACTUAL SIZE

A Height: ½ in (13 mm)
B Width: ½ in (13 mm)

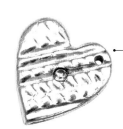

Gemstone heart *Press a fireable gemstone into the heart before drying and firing.*

Mirror shine *Make an untextured heart and polish to a mirror finish.*

Cutout heart *Cut out a smaller heart inside the main shape.*

4 Peel the clay off the texture sheet and place the clay, textured side up, onto a ceramic tile. Lay some plastic wrap over the clay.

5 Use a cutter to cut out a heart shape through the plastic wrap. This will round the edges to make an attractive domed heart shape.

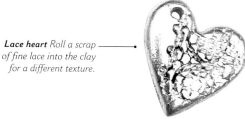

Lace heart *Roll a scrap of fine lace into the clay for a different texture.*

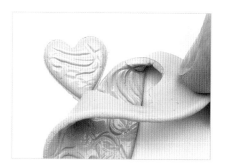

6 Carefully remove the plastic wrap and then the waste clay from around the cut shape, leaving the heart on the tile.

7 Use a fine yarn needle to make a pilot hole for hanging the charm, then dry the piece on the tile.

8 Sand away any rough edges and use a 1 mm drill bit to drill the hole neatly. Fire the piece and then brush and polish.

Stars

Star charms are quick and easy to make using widely available star cutters. You can make a variety of different charms using the same cutters. Those shown here are openwork stars that are attached using a jump ring or chain through the star. Alternatively, you can stack a small star onto a larger one for tiered stars that can be embellished with fireable gemstones.

Tools and materials

- Basic toolkit (see page 124)
- Silver clay: 5 g for rolling out (each star uses about 1 g)
- Star cutters: ³/₄ in (20 mm) and ³/₈ in (10 mm)
- Fireable gemstone: 3 mm round
- Peg and loop finding

OPENWORK STARS

1 Roll out a sheet of clay, 4 p.c. (1 mm) thick. Lay the sheet on a ceramic tile and smooth it down so that it sticks to the tile. Use the larger cutter to cut out a star, then remove the waste clay from around the shape.

2 Use the smaller cutter to cut a star inside the first star, lining up the points carefully.

3 Allow to air dry for a few minutes, then pierce the inner star with a darning needle held at a shallow angle and lift it clear. If there are any bits of clay left in the shape, leave them to be filed away after drying.

4 Dry the star on the tile and then file away any rough edges—be careful because the thin clay will be very fragile. Fire the star and then brush and polish.

STARS

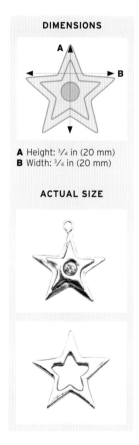

Plain star *Small mirror-polished stars set off the larger stars beautifully.*

Textured star *Roll lace onto the clay surface to texture it before cutting out star shapes, or texture the clay with a texture sheet.*

GEMSTONE STARS

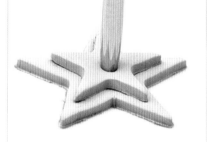

5 To make a gemstone star, roll out the clay as before and use the cutters to cut out one large and one small star. Brush water onto the back of the small star and then press it onto the center of the large star.

6 Use a large yarn needle to make a hole in the center of the small star for the stone. Holding the needle vertically, rotate it until the hole is just smaller in diameter than the stone.

7 Place the stone, flat top upward, in the hole and press down with tweezers until the top surface of the stone is just below the clay surface. Dry the star on the tile.

8 Sand and file away any rough edges. Use paste to attach a peg and loop finding to the back of one of the points and dry again. Fire the star but do not quench or the stone will shatter. Polish carefully to avoid damaging the stone.

DIMENSIONS

A
B

A Height: ³/₄ in (20 mm)
B Width: ³/₄ in (20 mm)

ACTUAL SIZE

Crosses

Maltese or Celtic cross charms are not difficult to make if you use tiny cutters to form the basic shapes. These can then be decorated and assembled into a cross in the plaster-dry stage. If you do not have a triangle cutter, make a paper template to cut around.

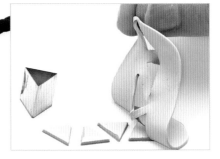

1 Roll out a sheet of clay, 4 p.c. (1 mm) thick. Lay this on a ceramic tile and use a cutter to cut out four triangles. Remove the waste clay from around the shapes.

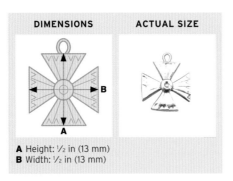

Tools and materials

- Basic toolkit (see page 124)
- Silver clay: 5 g for rolling out (Maltese cross uses 1.5 g; Celtic cross uses 2 g)
- Triangle cutter: 1/4 in (6 mm)
- Round cutter: 1/8 in (3 mm)
- Round cutters for Celtic cross ring (optional): 3/8 in (10 mm) and 1/4 in (6 mm)
- Ball-headed tool or knitting needle
- Peg and loop finding

DIMENSIONS	ACTUAL SIZE

A Height: 1/2 in (13 mm)
B Width: 1/2 in (13 mm)

2 Use a craft knife to mark each shape with lines radiating from one of the points. This will make the cross sparkle when it is polished.

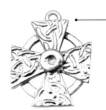

Decorated cross *Texture the clay using a Celtic design texture sheet before cutting out the triangles.*

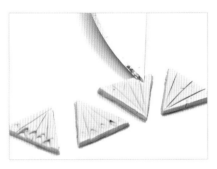

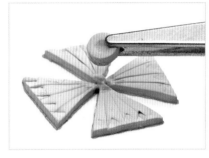

Long Celtic cross *Cut a longer triangle for the bottom of the cross using a straight blade. Oxidize the cross and then polish back to accentuate the details of the Celtic design.*

3 Use the triangular tip of the knife blade to impress little triangles along the outer edge of each triangle.

4 Roll out a small sheet of clay, 4 p.c. (1 mm) thick, and use the smallest round cutter to cut out a circle for the center of the cross. Use a ball tool or the tip of a knitting needle to indent the center of the circle.

5 Dry the pieces, then arrange the triangles into a cross shape with the central tips all touching. Apply paste to the center of the cross and then press the small circle on top. Dry again.

6 Use paste to attach a small peg and loop finding to the back of the cross. Reinforce the center with more paste between the triangles. Dry thoroughly and then sand away any rough edges.

7 Fire and brush the charm, then burnish the surface to bring out the sparkle.

8 To add a ring to the back of a Celtic cross, roll a sheet of clay, 4 p.c. (1 mm) thick, and use the two larger round cutters to cut out a ring (see page 56, step 2). Dry the ring and paste it onto the back of the cross before firing.

Padlocks

Padlock charms are eternally popular and finish off a chain bracelet to perfection. These little padlocks have decorative screws, but you can make padlocks of all shapes and sizes and decorate them in many different ways.

Tools and materials

- Basic toolkit (see page 124)
- Silver clay: 5 g for rolling out (each padlock uses 1.5 g)
- Square cutter: ³/₈ in (10 mm), or use a straight blade
- Toothpick with the end cut off neatly
- 2 mm screwdriver or a 2 mm wide strip of stiff cardstock

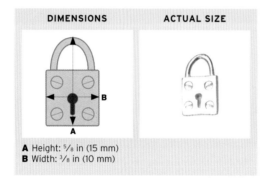

DIMENSIONS   **ACTUAL SIZE**

A Height: ⁵/₈ in (15 mm)
B Width: ³/₈ in (10 mm)

1 First make the shackle (top loop) of the padlock. Roll a log of clay, ¹/₁₆ in (1.5 mm) thick and about 1 in (25 mm) long.

2 Curve the log into a semicircle, ³/₈ in (10 mm) across and the same high. Trim the ends and dry.

3 Roll out a sheet of clay, 6 p.c. (1.5 mm) thick, and place on a ceramic tile.

4 Use a square cutter or straight blade to cut a ³/₈ in (10 mm) square of clay. Remove the waste clay.

Heart padlock Use a ½ in (13 mm) heart cutter for the padlock body.

Padlock and key — Make a key charm (see page 28) and attach it to the padlock with a short length of silver chain.

Textured padlock Texture the clay after rolling out to give a decorative padlock. Oxidize and then polish back to accentuate the textured design.

Flower key Cute little key variation with a tiny flower as the bit (see page 28).

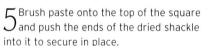

5 Brush paste onto the top of the square and push the ends of the dried shackle into it to secure in place.

6 Suggest four screw heads by pushing the cut end of a toothpick into the clay a little way in from each corner. Mark each circle indent at an angle with the end of a 2 mm screwdriver.

7 Make a keyhole in the lower center of the padlock using a large yarn needle to form the round upper hole and the screwdriver to form the lower slot.

8 Dry the padlock and then reinforce the shackle joins with paste. Dry again, sand smooth if required, and fire. Polish or leave with a satin finish. Attach a jump ring to the shackle for hanging.

Keys

Tiny keys make delightful charms in their own right or to combine with the little padlocks on page 26. They can be made with all kinds of decorative bows (the part you hold) and bits (the part that goes into the lock), so great variety is possible. Try making a tiny bunch of key charms, threaded onto a ring of wire, for a unique pendant.

Tools and materials

- Basic toolkit (see page 124)
- Silver clay: 3 g for rolling out (each key uses 1 g or less)
- Flower cutter: 1/4 in (6 mm)

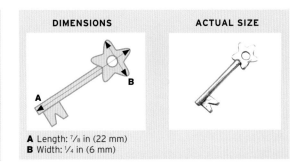

DIMENSIONS | ACTUAL SIZE

A Length: 7/8 in (22 mm)
B Width: 1/4 in (6 mm)

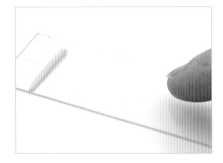

1 Roll a log of clay, 1 in (25 mm) long and 1/8 in (3 mm) thick. Place a log roller over it and continue rolling back and forth until the log is about 1/16 in (1.5 mm) thick.

2 Lay the log on a ceramic tile and push a straight edge against it. This will help to straighten the log for drying.

3 To make the bow of the key, roll out a small sheet of clay, 4 p.c. (1 mm) thick, and smooth onto a tile. Use a cutter to cut out a flower shape, carefully removing the waste clay from around it.

Filigree bow Use a small heart cutter to cut out the bow and then pierce with three holes to make a heart-shaped filigree bow.

Decorative bit Use a needle file to file notches out of the sides of the bit.

Round bow Use a tiny ³/₁₆ in (5 mm) flower cutter to cut out the hole in a round bow.

4 To make a hole in the bow, push the tip of a large yarn needle into the center of the flower and, holding the needle vertically, rotate it to enlarge the hole.

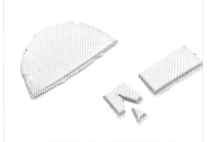

5 Roll out another small sheet of clay, 2 p.c. (0.5 mm) thick, and use a straight blade to cut a ³/₁₆ in (5 mm) square. Use a craft knife to cut out a V shape from one side.

6 Dry all the pieces. Trim the shank to ⁵/₈ in (15 mm), then use a fine file or sanding pad to smooth all the pieces carefully. The tiny pieces are relatively thin and may snap if treated roughly.

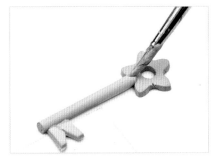

7 Use generous dabs of paste to join the parts of the key together, supporting the bit on the edge of a 2 p.c. (0.5 mm) rolling guide so that the bit is held in the center of the shank. Dry again and sand away any excess.

8 Fire the key and then brush and burnish to a shine. The charm can be hung by attaching a jump ring through the bow of the key.

Lucky clovers

Charms are often connected with luck and the four-leaf clover is a traditional good luck charm. This project shows you how to create a dainty four-leaf clover and then color it with resin.

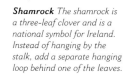

Shamrock *The shamrock is a three-leaf clover and is a national symbol for Ireland. Instead of hanging by the stalk, add a separate hanging loop behind one of the leaves.*

Tools and materials

- Basic toolkit (see page 124)
- Silver clay: 5 g for rolling out (each clover uses 1 g)
- Heart cutter: ¼ in (6 mm)
- Round cutter: ³⁄₁₆ in (5 mm)
- Pure silver wire: 1 in (25 mm) length of 20 gauge (0.8 mm) wire
- Two-part clear coating resin
- Green oil paint or resin pigment
- Mixing cup and spatula
- Rubbing alcohol and cotton swab
- Glass tumbler

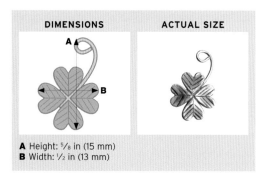

DIMENSIONS	ACTUAL SIZE

A Height: ⅝ in (15 mm)
B Width: ½ in (13 mm)

1 Roll out the clay, 2 p.c. (0.5 mm) thick, and place on a ceramic tile. Use cutters to cut out four hearts and one circle. Carefully remove the waste clay from around the shapes.

2 Use the blade of a craft knife to mark a central rib and veins on each heart-shaped leaf.

LUCKY CLOVERS

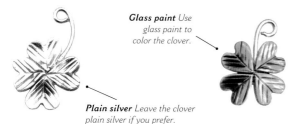

Glass paint *Use glass paint to color the clover.*

Plain silver *Leave the clover plain silver if you prefer.*

Stalk *You can make the stalk longer or shorter, and vary its curve and loop as you wish.*

Color tints *Try tinting the resin with different greens by mixing touches of yellow or blue oil paint into the green resin.*

3 Press one end of the silver wire down onto the circle of clay, with the end of the wire positioned at the center of the circle. Brush paste over the circle.

4 Use tweezers to arrange the four leaves on the circle, points to the center and trapping the wire between. Press down over the leaves to ensure a good join, then dry the piece on the tile. Use sanding pads to smooth any rough edges and then fire, brush, and polish.

5 Use round-nose pliers to turn a loop on the end of the wire. The charm can be hung by attaching a jump ring through this loop.

6 Mix a small quantity (1 ml is plenty) of the two parts of the resin according to the instructions on the package. Scoop a little of the mixture onto a ceramic tile and add a match-head size dab of oil paint. Use a large yarn needle to stir the paint into the resin thoroughly.

7 Use a cotton swab to clean the surface of the leaf with alcohol and allow to dry. This degreases the surface so that the resin will adhere well.

8 Apply a thin coat of resin to the leaf with the needle. Do not apply too much or it will flow off the leaf. Place the leaf on a level surface with an upside down glass tumbler over it to keep dust off and allow the resin to set (usually about 24 hours).

32

Tools and materials

- Basic toolkit (see page 124)
- Silver clay: 3 g for rolling out (each horseshoe uses 1.5 g or less)
- Circle cutter: ³⁄₈ in (10 mm)

Horseshoes

Horseshoes are a popular symbol of good luck. They are sometimes seen with the attachment loop at the bottom of the horseshoe, but this means that the luck will fall out, so here they are attached at the top. You can buy molds to make horseshoe charms, but they are very easy to make yourself.

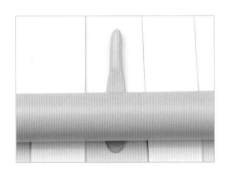

1 Shape the clay into a log, about ¹⁄₄ in (6 mm) thick. Lay this between 6 p.c. (1.5 mm) rolling guides and roll out into a long strip.

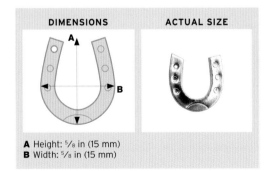

DIMENSIONS

ACTUAL SIZE

A Height: ⁵⁄₈ in (15 mm)
B Width: ⁵⁄₈ in (15 mm)

2 Use a straight blade to cut a strip, ¹⁄₈ in (3 mm) wide and about 2 in (50 mm) long.

3 Place the strip on a tile and pull the ends toward you, coaxing the strip into a U shape. Place the circle cutter inside the curve and continue to ease the two ends of the strip around this to form a symmetrical horseshoe shape.

Hearts horseshoe *Use a ³⁄₁₆ in (5 mm) heart cutter to cut out two tiny hearts from a 4 p.c. (1 mm) thick sheet of clay. Use paste to attach the overlapping hearts to the bottom of the horseshoe.*

Attachment loop *Instead of drilling through one of the nail holes, push a peg and loop finding into one end of the horseshoe for hanging the charm.*

Birthday horseshoe *Press a fireable gemstone of the correct color (see page 105) into the bottom of the horseshoe before drying and firing.*

4 Use a craft knife to trim the ends at an angle. If any cracks appear on the outside of the curve, wet a finger and rub it over the cracks to slick them away. Deep cracks indicate that the clay was too dry, in which case it is best to rehydrate the clay and re-roll.

5 Use the flat end of a 1 mm drill bit to impress nail holes evenly spaced along each side the horseshoe. Leave a gap at the center where nails are not used.

6 Decide which way you want the horseshoe to hang and use the tip of a fine yarn needle to make one of the holes at the end deeper; this will be drilled through later for attaching a jump ring.

7 Mark a small curve at the bottom of the horseshoe with the circle cutter. Dry the piece on the tile and then sand away any rough edges if required.

8 Use the 1 mm drill bit to drill the hole for the jump ring, then fire and polish the horseshoe.

Coins

Coins drilled with a hole for hanging have long been used as charms all over the world. This project shows how to create charms in silver clay using molds made from existing coins. Simple one-part push molds made in polymer clay replicate the details of coins extremely accurately. You can replicate coins found in antique stores, coins from a favorite foreign vacation, or a coin with the appropriate year for a child's birth.

Tools and materials

- Basic toolkit (see page 124)
- Silver clay: 2 g per coin (quantity will vary according to size of coin being molded)
- Small coin: the coin shown is a commercial replica of a Roman coin
- Polymer clay: about ¼ of a 2 oz (56 g) block
- Talcum powder

1 Knead the polymer clay in your hands until it is really soft and pliable. Shape the clay into a ball and press it down onto a ceramic tile to make a patty about ¼ in (6 mm) thick and large enough to mold the coin with about ¼ in (6 mm) extra all around.

2 Smear the surface of the patty with talcum powder—this is to prevent the coin from sticking in the clay. Press the chosen side of the coin firmly into the clay until the clay surface is level with the top of the coin all around.

DIMENSIONS	ACTUAL SIZE
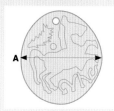	

A Diameter: ⁵⁄₈ in (15 mm)

COINS

Antique coin To make a coin look antique, oxidize and then polish back to accentuate the details of the design.

Color range Oxidize coins for varying amounts of time to achieve a range of colors, from gold and copper to blue and purple. Varnish the coins to prevent the colors from rubbing off.

Double-sided Push the other side of the original coin onto the silver clay in the mold before demolding.

3 Push the clay back toward the coin if it pulls away. With the coin still embedded, bake the polymer clay as recommended on the package. Allow to cool and then remove the coin.

4 To mold a coin in silver clay, form a ball of silver clay about half the diameter of the mold cavity. Flatten the ball slightly into a disk and smear one side with oil to prevent it from sticking to the mold.

5 Press the disk into the center of the mold with your fingertip held flat until the clay spreads to fill the cavity. Smooth the surface of the clay with your finger to remove any fold lines or blemishes.

6 Leave the clay in the mold for about five minutes to let it dry and harden slightly, then tip it out of the mold. If the silver clay is difficult to remove, pierce the back with a darning needle held at a shallow angle and ease it out. The small hole can then be smoothed away.

7 Use a fine yarn needle to make a pilot hole in the coin about ¹⁄₁₆ in (1.5 mm) from the edge for hanging the charm. Dry the coin fully and then sand the edges and back to smooth them. Drill the hole with a 1 mm drill bit.

8 Fire the coin, then brush and burnish. The detail of the relief design on the coin will be reproduced very clearly.

Tools and materials

- Basic toolkit (see page 124)
- Silver clay: 5 g for rolling out several charms (each flower uses about 0.5 g)
- Rubber stamp: an all-over floral pattern is used here
- Flower cutter: 3/8 in (10 mm)
- Bamboo skewer or length of wooden dowel: 1/8 in (3 mm) diameter
- Two-part clear coating resin
- Oil paint or resin pigment in assorted colors
- Mixing cup and spatula
- Rubbing alcohol and cotton swab
- Glass tumbler

Flowers

Flowers are an eternal favorite and you can make a colorful variety of flower charms using resin to create the effect of enamel. This project shows how to use rubber stamps and simple flower cutters to create the charms. Choose stamps with bold flower patterns or geometric all-over designs to add to the variety.

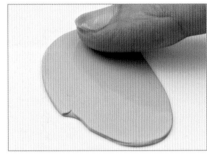

1 Roll out a sheet of clay, 4 p.c. (1 mm) thick, and place on a ceramic tile. Lightly oil one side.

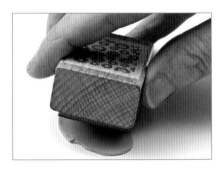

2 Press the rubber stamp down onto the clay surface, pressing sufficiently to make an impression. Do not press too hard or the stamp will go right through the clay.

FLOWERS

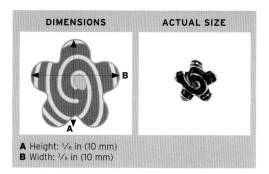

DIMENSIONS

ACTUAL SIZE

A Height: ³/₈ in (10 mm)
B Width: ³/₈ in (10 mm)

Leaves Leaves can be made in the same way using a heart or diamond cutter. Color the leaves with green resin.

Briar rose Omit the texture and draw lines between the petals in the soft clay. Mark the center with small dots.

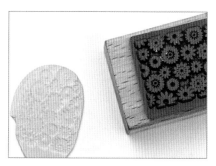

3 Check the impression; it should be deep enough to show as a clear impression but without leaving the clay too thin. If you are not happy with the result, fold the clay in half and roll again.

4 Use a cutter to cut out flower shapes from the stamped sheet, choosing appropriate points in the impressed pattern that suggest flower shapes and petals radiating from the center. Carefully remove the waste clay.

5 Accentuate the center of each flower by pressing the flat end of a skewer into it. This center impression will help to define the flower. If the clay cracks a little, brush with a dampened paintbrush.

6 Use a fine yarn needle to make a pilot hole near the edge of a petal for hanging each charm, then dry the flowers thoroughly. Sand away any rough edges.

7 Use a 1 mm drill bit to drill the hole, then fire the pieces. Brush well to get into all the details of the impressed pattern and then burnish.

8 Color the flowers with resin in the colors of your choice (see page 31, steps 6–8). A small dab of yellow resin in the center of each flower draws charms with different textures together into a set.

Rosebud on stalk *Make a smaller rose with fewer petal coils and roll a separate thin log of clay for the stalk or stem. Paste a tiny leaf onto the stalk. Dry the rosebud and then drill a hole into the base and paste one end of the stalk into it. Dry again, then add a peg and loop finding and fire.*

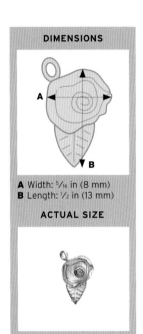

DIMENSIONS

A Width: 5/16 in (8 mm)
B Length: 1/2 in (13 mm)

ACTUAL SIZE

Tools and materials

- Basic toolkit (see page 124)
- Silver clay: 1.5–2 g per rose
- Sharp scissors
- Peg and loop finding

Roses

Roses speak of love and are one of the most adored flowers. These little rose charms are hand sculpted so that no two will ever be exactly the same. Make sure that the clay is well hydrated before you begin or the petals will dry too quickly for successful forming. Try making the roses in polymer clay first to practice the technique.

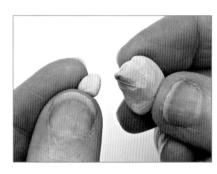

1 Pull off a small piece of clay and form into a ball, about 1/4 in (6 mm) diameter or the approximate size that you want the rose to be.

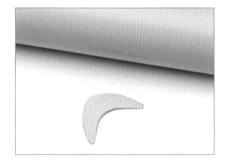

2 Form the ball into a log, about 2 in (5 cm) long and tapered at both ends. Lay it on a non-stick surface in a U shape and use a roller to flatten the log into a crescent-shaped strip, about 1/4 in (6 mm) wide and 2 p.c. (0.5 mm) thick or less.

ROSES

Extra leaves *Try adding two leaves for a more symmetrical charm.*

3 Peel the strip off the surface and pinch all along the outer edge to frill it slightly and thin it further.

4 Brush water on the strip and then roll it up from one end—this will be the center of the rose. Continue rolling to the other end of the strip, arranging the last few rolls to be lower down the rose and more opened out.

5 Squeeze the base of the rose to secure the layers, and pull out the outer petals a little to shape the flower.

6 Use scissors to trim the base of the rose so that it has a flat back. The rose should only be about ³/₁₆ in (5 mm) deep. Dry thoroughly.

7 Form an ¹/₈ in (3 mm) ball of clay into a teardrop shape and then press it onto a ceramic tile to flatten it into a leaf shape. Use the blade of a craft knife to mark veins on the leaf. Wet the rounded end of the leaf and press the flat back of the rose firmly onto it. Dry on the tile.

8 Use a 1 mm drill bit to drill a hole in the side of the rose for hanging, positioning the hole so that the leaf will hang down at an angle. Insert a peg and loop finding, using paste to secure it. Fire the rose, then brush and burnish.

Shells

Making molds for charms is a fascinating way of replicating natural objects, and the varied textures and lovely shapes of seashells make them particularly satisfying to turn into beautiful charms. You can mold shells from a particular vacation as a memento, or make a collection of shell charms for a sea-themed bracelet. The molds in this project are made using putty silicone, which sets relatively flexible for easy removal of the molded silver clay.

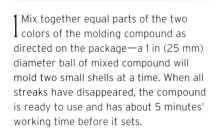

1 Mix together equal parts of the two colors of the molding compound as directed on the package—a 1 in (25 mm) diameter ball of mixed compound will mold two small shells at a time. When all streaks have disappeared, the compound is ready to use and has about 5 minutes' working time before it sets.

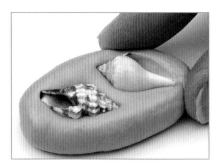

2 Shape the compound into an oval ball and then flatten slightly into a patty. Press the shells into the compound until it comes about halfway up the sides of each shell. Push the compound against the sides of the shells if it pulls away.

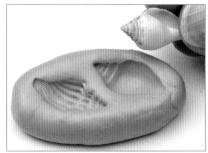

3 Leave the mold to set for the time recommended on the package. Test for setting by pressing a fingernail into the side of the mold. When no impression can be made, remove the shells from the mold.

SHELLS

Shell shapes *Many different shell types can be molded using this technique. When molding a flat shell such as a cockle, press the silver clay into the deep part of the mold and work it toward the edges.*

DIMENSIONS	ACTUAL SIZE
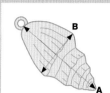 B A	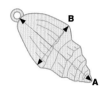

A Length: ⅝ in (15 mm)
B Width: ⁵⁄₁₆ in (8 mm)

4 Form a ball of silver clay, a little less than half the size of the original shell. Smooth away any fold lines or these will show in the molded piece. Shape the clay so that it is roughly the same shape as the mold cavity. Smooth a light smear of oil over the surface of the clay to prevent sticking and press into the mold.

5 Push the clay to the edges of the cavity, making the surface slightly concave. Do not let it spread beyond the mold cavity or it will need a lot of trimming later. Decorate the back of the charm by pressing the original shell into the back of the clay, aligning it in the same way as the cavity.

Adding a pearl *Mold two cockleshells and paste them together so that they are slightly open, with a peg and loop finding inserted between for hanging. After firing and polishing, glue a freshwater pearl inside.*

Tools and materials

- Basic toolkit (see page 124)
- Silver clay: 1.5 g per shell (quantity will vary according to size of shell being molded)
- Seashells: choose small shells, ¾ in (20 mm) or less, with plenty of texture and pleasing shapes
- Putty silicone molding compound
- Peg and loop finding

6 Leave the piece for a few minutes to dry and then flex the mold to turn out the clay. If the molding is not successful, reshape the clay and mold again.

7 Push a peg and loop finding into the clay at the base of the shell for hanging the charm. Dry the shell, then fire and polish.

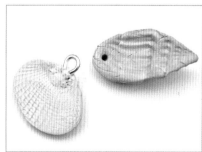

8 Flat shells such as cockleshells can have the peg and loop finding pasted to the underside if the shell is not thick enough for piercing. Alternatively, make a pilot hole through the molded shell with a fine yarn needle. Dry the shell and then drill the hole with a 1 mm bit.

Butterflies

Tiny butterflies fluttering around your wrist make a delightful bracelet. Use a variety of colors for the wings or intermingle with flower and leaf charms for a country meadow bracelet. Skeleton leaves are used to texture the clay surface for the wings, which are then cut out using heart cutters.

Tools and materials

- Basic toolkit (see page 124)
- Silver clay: 5 g for rolling out (each butterfly uses about 1 g)
- Small heart cutter: 5/16 in (8 mm) is used here, but slightly larger—such as 3/8 in (10 mm)— would also be fine
- Small skeleton leaves (available from craft stores) or real leaves to texture the clay
- Peg and loop finding
- Rubbing alcohol and cotton swab
- Transparent colored inks
- Varnish suitable for metal

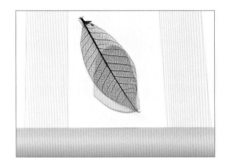

1 Roll out the clay, 4 p.c. (1 mm) thick, and smear the surface with oil. Lay a skeleton leaf on the clay and then roll again between the rolling guides to texture the surface. Peel off the leaf.

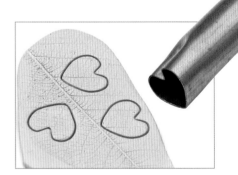

2 Place the textured sheet onto a ceramic tile, smoothing it down lightly to stick it to the tile. Use a cutter to cut out three heart shapes, with the impressed leaf veins fanning out on each. Carefully remove the waste clay.

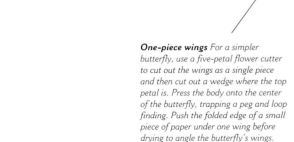

One-piece wings For a simpler butterfly, use a five-petal flower cutter to cut out the wings as a single piece and then cut out a wedge where the top petal is. Press the body onto the center of the butterfly, trapping a peg and loop finding. Push the folded edge of a small piece of paper under one wing before drying to angle the butterfly's wings.

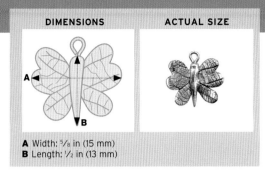

DIMENSIONS | **ACTUAL SIZE**

A Width: ⅝ in (15 mm)
B Length: ½ in (13 mm)

BUTTERFLIES

Wing shape Arrange four half heart pieces, the top two with points outward, to make different shaped wings.

Size variation Use heart cutters of different sizes to make larger or smaller butterflies.

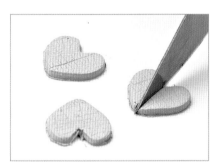

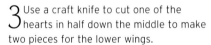

3 Use a craft knife to cut one of the hearts in half down the middle to make two pieces for the lower wings.

4 Dry the pieces and then use paste to attach the cut side of each half heart to the side of one of the whole hearts to make two butterfly wings. Dry again.

5 Form an ⅛ in (3 mm) ball of clay and roll into a tapered log for the butterfly body. Trim off the thick end to leave a tapered body ½ in (13 mm) long. Push a peg and loop finding into the thicker end of the tapered body.

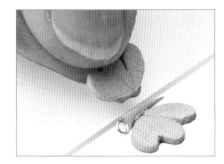

6 Apply paste to the inside of each wing and press onto either side of the body. For a realistic effect, position the second wing at an angle and support it with a rolling guide or playing cards. Dry thoroughly and then reinforce the back with paste to make a strong join.

7 Sand or file away any rough edges and then dry again. Fire the butterfly, then brush and burnish.

8 Use a cotton swab to clean the surface of the butterfly with alcohol and allow to dry. Paint with colored inks, letting the ink settle into the textured pattern to accentuate it. When the ink has dried, paint over each butterfly with varnish to preserve the color.

Bead dangles Make toadstool bead dangles (see page 141) using a red flower bead for the cap and a couple of small clear beads for the stem.

Toadstools

Tiny toadstools for fairies to sit on make dainty charms with a pretty shape. Toadstools can be combined with fairy and pumpkin coach charms to make a fairy tale bracelet (see page 48). This project shows how to sculpt toadstools directly in silver clay, but you could sculpt them in polymer clay instead, which is easier to work with than silver clay, and then create a mold if you prefer.

Tools and materials

- Basic toolkit (see page 124)
- Silver clay: 1 g per toadstool

SCULPTED TOADSTOOL

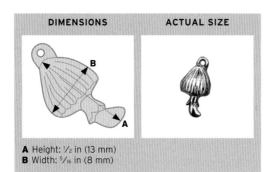

DIMENSIONS   **ACTUAL SIZE**

A Height: 1/2 in (13 mm)
B Width: 5/16 in (8 mm)

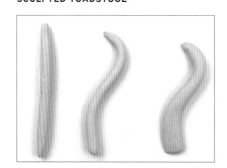

1 Roll a log of clay, 1/16 in (1.5 mm) thick and about 1 in (25 mm) long. Form the log into a shallow S-shaped curve and press down lightly onto a ceramic tile. Flatten the bottom 1/4 in (6 mm) of the log a little for the stem of the toadstool.

2 Form a 1/4 in (6 mm) ball of clay and point the top a little. Press the ball down onto the tile to shape the clay into the toadstool cap. Push the blade of a craft knife against the bottom of the cap to flatten it, and pinch the top into a gentle curve.

TOADSTOOLS

Colored toadstool
Use glass paint to paint the toadstool cap for a more colorful charm.

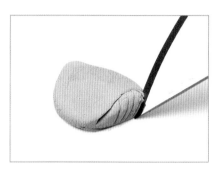

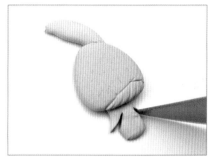

Texture *Try varying the texture of the toadstool cap. Vertical lines or stippling with a darning needle give interesting effects.*

3 Mark gills on the bottom of the cap with the knife blade. Slide the blade under the cap to remove it from the tile.

4 Brush water onto the center of the stem and press the cap onto it about 1/8 in (3 mm) from the bottom. The rest of the stem will protrude at the top to be made into a hanging loop. Make a shallow cut on each side of the foot of the stem and curve a sliver of cut clay upward to suggest a spiky ring around the stem.

5 Mark lines on the center of the stem to continue the spiky ring. Trim off the top of the protruding clay stem, smooth the cut end into a rounded shape, and pierce with a fine yarn needle to make a pilot hole for the hanging loop.

MOLDED TOADSTOOL

6 Roll tiny balls of clay and flatten between your fingers. Brush water over the cap and then press on the flattened balls for a spotty toadstool.

7 Dry thoroughly on the tile and then use a 1 mm drill bit to drill the hanging hole. Fire, brush, and polish.

8 For an easier project, sculpt toadstools in polymer clay and then make a mold from the baked piece to replicate in silver. You can make the mold in polymer clay (see page 34) or putty silicone (see page 40).

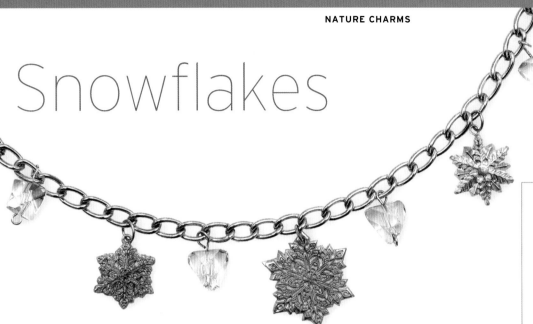

Snowflakes

Icy bead dangles *Intersperse the silver clay snowflakes with clear glass bead dangles (see page 141) to resemble chunks of ice.*

Snowflakes and silver are a perfect combination. This easy project uses plastic novelty buttons in the form of snowflakes; these are widely available from sewing notion stores, craft shops, and scrapbook suppliers. A simple mold in polymer clay is made from the buttons to replicate them in pure silver.

1 Knead the polymer clay in your hands until it is really soft and pliable. Form it into an oval shape and press it down onto a ceramic tile to make a patty a little larger than the snowflake button. Smear the surface of the patty with talcum powder to prevent sticking.

2 Press the button, right side down, into the center of the clay patty and push gently until the surrounding clay is level with the back of the button.

3 Use a darning needle to ease the button out of the clay, or pull firmly on the protruding button shank if there is one. Bake the polymer clay as recommended on the package.

SNOWFLAKES

Earrings Snowflakes make lovely earrings. Make a pair of matching snowflakes and attach a fish hook earwire to each.

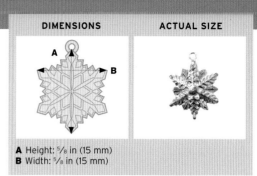

DIMENSIONS	ACTUAL SIZE

A Height: ⅝ in (15 mm)
B Width: ⅝ in (15 mm)

Tools and materials

- Basic toolkit (see page 124)
- Silver clay: 2 g or less per snowflake (quantity will vary according to size of original button being molded)
- Polymer clay: about ¼ of a 2 oz (56 g) block
- Plastic snowflake buttons or scrapbook embellishments: choose pieces that have good textured detail and shapes that are not too deeply cut
- Talcum powder
- Peg and loop finding

4 When the mold is cool, form a ball of silver clay about half the diameter of the mold cavity. Smear one side of the ball with oil and then press the ball, oiled side down, into the mold. Keep pressing until the cavity is filled to the edges.

5 Smooth the back of the clay surface with your finger and then push the original button onto the clay, aligning it with the mold's points (you may find it helpful to mark these with permanent marker) to indent a snowflake pattern on the back of the clay.

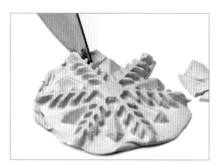

6 Leave the clay in the mold for five minutes to harden slightly, then ease it out of the mold. If it is difficult to remove, use a darning needle (see page 35, step 6). Lay the snowflake on the tile and trim away excess clay from around the edges.

7 Dry the snowflake and then file away any rough edges. You can file into tight corners easily with a fine needle file.

8 Paste a peg and loop finding onto one of the snowflake's points. Fire the snowflake, then brush and polish.

Antique snowflake Oxidize the charm and then polish back to accentuate the detail of the design.

Fairies

Tools and materials

- Basic toolkit (see page 124)
- Silver clay: 1 g per fairy
- Polymer clay (for sculpting fairy): about ⅛ of a 2 oz (56 g) block
- Polymer clay and talcum powder (for making mold), or putty silicone molding compound
- Peg and loop finding

Tiny fairies will charm any little girl. This project involves miniature sculpting, which is easiest to do when working flat on a ceramic tile. Silver clay is demanding to sculpt because it dries so quickly, so it is best to sculpt complex designs such as this in polymer clay and then make a mold.

Fairytale bracelet
Combine fairy charms with toadstool and pumpkin coach charms (see pages 44 and 50), alternated with crystal dangles (see page 141).

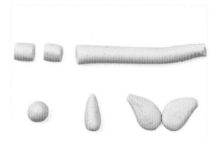

1 Roll a log of polymer clay, ⅛ in (3 mm) thick, and cut two ⅛ in (3 mm) lengths. Roll each one into a ball, then point one end to make a teardrop. Arrange these on a ceramic tile, points angled outward and upward, and press down to make wings.

2 Form a log of clay, 1/32 in (1 mm) thick and ½ in (13 mm) long, and roll the ends to taper them. Use a craft knife to cut the log in half for the fairy's legs and arrange them side by side, points downward, just below the wings.

3 Form a ³/₁₆ in (5 mm) ball of clay, then point one end to make a teardrop shape. Press the teardrop onto a tile, point upward, until it is only about 4 p.c. (1 mm) thick to make the fairy's dress. Cut the bottom of the dress into points.

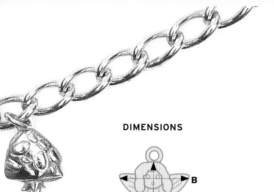

DIMENSIONS

A Height: ¹/₂ in (13 mm)
B Width: ³/₈ in (10 mm)

ACTUAL SIZE

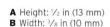

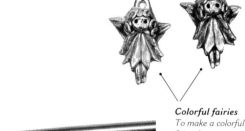

Colorful fairies
To make a colorful fairy charm bracelet, apply tinted resin to the dresses and wings.

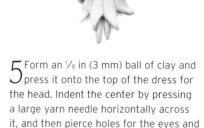

4 Slice the dress off the tile and press it onto the wings and legs so that the top of the dress is just between the wings. Use the knife to mark veins on the wings and lines on the dress. Make arms in the same way as the legs, but thinner, and press onto the top of the dress.

5 Form an ¹/₈ in (3 mm) ball of clay and press it onto the top of the dress for the head. Indent the center by pressing a large yarn needle horizontally across it, and then pierce holes for the eyes and mouth with the point of a darning needle.

Angel *Alter the shape of the wings, omit the legs, and make the dress long. The loop of the peg and loop finding doubles as a halo.*

6 Make a long thin log, as thin as you can (see page 128), and coil into loops around the head for the hair, pressing the loops down lightly to secure. Bake the fairy on the tile as recommended on the package.

7 Make a mold of the hardened fairy using either polymer clay (see page 34) or putty silicone (see page 40). To make a silver fairy charm, form a ¹/₄ in (6 mm) ball of silver clay, oil the surface of the ball lightly, and press it into the mold cavity.

8 Remove from the mold and trim away any excess clay from around the edges if necessary (see page 47, step 6). Push a peg and loop finding into the top of the fairy's head. Dry, then fire and polish.

Pumpkin coaches

Tools and materials

- Basic toolkit (see page 124)
- Silver clay: 1 g per coach
- Polymer clay: about ⅛ of a 2 oz (56 g) block
- Putty silicone molding compound
- Brush protector or round cutter: ⅛ in (3 mm)

Fairy tale charms add a touch of magic to jewelry for children and the young at heart. This little pumpkin coach can be made as part of a themed bracelet. Combine with fairy and toadstool charms, or any other charms you fancy such as flowers or snowflakes. Finish with occasional sparkly bead dangles for a magical bracelet. It is easier to make the coach in polymer clay and then use this to make a mold.

1 Form a ¼ in (6 mm) ball of polymer clay and shape it into an oval. Press it down onto a ceramic tile, flattening it with your finger until it is about ⅜ in (10 mm) across, to make the pumpkin body.

2 Mark vertical lines on the pumpkin with a fine yarn needle, curving the lines to follow the shape of the pumpkin. Push the blade of a craft knife into the top of the pumpkin to indent it.

PUMPKIN COACHES

DIMENSIONS **ACTUAL SIZE**

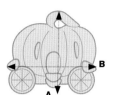

A Height: 3/8 in (10 mm)
B Length: 5/8 in (15 mm)

Golden coach
*Oxidize the coach
until the color becomes
a light gold. Varnish to
preserve the finish.*

Pumpkin orange
*This coach has
been oxidized for
longer than the
golden one to turn
it a deep orange
pumpkin color.*

3 Roll a 1/16 in (1.5 mm) thick log of clay and push one end into the top of the pumpkin. Curve the other end around and trim to about 3/16 in (5 mm) long. Press the cut end down onto the body of the pumpkin to form a loop.

4 Push the knife blade against the bottom of the pumpkin to straighten it. Press the remainder of the clay log against the bottom of the pumpkin for the axle, trimming it at each end at the edges of the pumpkin.

5 Form two 1/16 in (1.5 mm) balls of clay and press one onto each end of the axle for the wheels. Keep pressing with the flat pad of your finger until each wheel is a little larger than 1/8 in (3 mm).

6 Press the end of a brush protector or round cutter onto the center of each wheel to suggest a tire. Mark spokes with the tip of the knife.

7 Use the needle to mark a door and two windows. Cut slices from a thin log of clay and press them with the knife onto each end of the pumpkin for fenders. Apply two thinner slices below the door to suggest steps.

8 Bake the coach on the tile as recommended on the package. When it is cool, make a mold using putty silicone and then mold a pumpkin coach in silver clay (see page 40). Alternatively, make a polymer clay mold (see page 34).

Flying kites

Tiny silver kites with a shower of colored bows for their tails make lively charms. Polymer clay is used to make the bows, which are then attached to a fine silver chain.

Tools and materials

- Basic toolkit (see page 124)
- Silver clay: 3 g for rolling out (each kite uses 1 g)
- Graph paper for template
- Silver chain: you will need a 1 in (25 mm) length that can be cut from a longer chain when making the tail; use a fine chain with links that are large enough for attaching a jump ring—fine rolo or belcher chain is ideal
- Polymer clay: small pieces in two bright colors
- Jump rings: two 4 mm fine-gauge rings

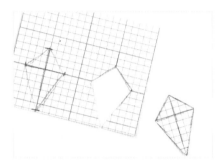

1 Make a template for the kite using graph paper. Mark a kite shape centered on crossing lines on the graph paper, with ¼ in (6 mm) above the horizontal line, ½ in (13 mm) below it, and ¼ in (6 mm) on either side of the vertical central line. Cut out the template.

2 Roll out the silver clay, 4 p.c. (1 mm) thick, and lay it on a ceramic tile. Lay the template on the clay and use a straight blade to cut out the shape.

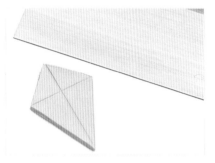

3 Use the back of the straight blade to mark vertical and horizontal lines joining the points of the kite. Slide the blade under the kite and flip it over to repeat the lines on the back.

DIMENSIONS   **ACTUAL SIZE**

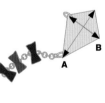

A Length: ¾ in (20 mm)
B Width: ½ in (13 mm)

FLYING KITES

Kite shape *Alter the shape of the kite. Here, the top is trimmed into a curve.*

Beaded tail *Thread tiny colored beads onto headpins and attach to the chain for a jeweled kite tail.*

4 Use a fine yarn needle to make pilot holes in the bottom point and one of the side points of the kite. Dry the piece and then drill the holes with a 1 mm drill bit. Sand any rough areas, then fire and polish.

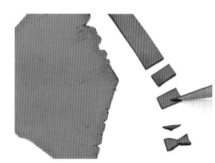

5 Roll out two colors of polymer clay, 2 p.c. (0.5 mm) thick, and cut ⅛ x ³⁄₁₆ in (3 x 5 mm) rectangles for the bows on the kite tail. Use a craft knife to cut out a V shape from the long sides of each rectangle to make little bow shapes.

6 Lay the bows in a row on a tile, evenly spaced about ¼ in (6 mm) apart. Press the silver chain onto the bows, with one end of the chain extending about ¼ in (6 mm) beyond the first bow. Press small strips of polymer clay onto the back of each bow to trap the chain.

7 Bake the chain with the polymer clay bows on the tile as recommended on the package. Cool and free from the tile by sliding a blade under the bows. Use wire cutters to trim the long end of the chain by cutting the link just beyond the last bow.

8 Using fine-nose pliers, attach the end of the chain to the hole in the bottom of the kite with a jump ring. The charm can be hung by attaching a second jump ring through the side point of the kite.

CHILDREN'S CHARMS

Tools and materials

- Basic toolkit
  (see page 124)
- Silver clay: 2.5 g per
  teddy bear
- Peg and loop finding

Teddy bears

Every child has a teddy bear, so this little charm has wide appeal. The charm is sculpted in 3-D, so it is a complete little figure. Practice making the teddy in polymer clay first, and make sure that the silver clay is well hydrated before you begin. Brush water onto the clay with a paintbrush whenever you want to add a fresh piece to help it stick.

DIMENSIONS

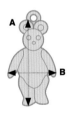

A Height: ⁵⁄₈ in (15 mm)
B Width: ¹⁄₄ in (6 mm)

ACTUAL SIZE

1 Roll a log of clay, ¹⁄₈ in (3 mm) thick, and cut two ¹⁄₄ in (6 mm) lengths for the legs. Shape one end of each cut log into a simple foot and pinch the other end to flatten it slightly for the top of the leg.

2 Form a ⁵⁄₁₆ in (8 mm) ball of clay and shape it into an oval. Pinch the bottom to point it a little. Brush the inner tops of the legs with water and press the wetted area onto the bottom of the body on each side.

TEDDY BEARS

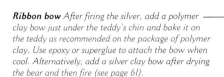

Ribbon bow *After firing the silver, add a polymer clay bow just under the teddy's chin and bake it on the teddy as recommended on the package of polymer clay. Use epoxy or superglue to attach the bow when cool. Alternatively, add a silver clay bow after drying the bear and then fire (see page 61).*

Sitting teddy *Make the legs seated by laying them on the tile in a V shape. Press the body onto the top of the legs and continue as for the standing teddy.*

3 Roll another log, 1/16 in (1.5 mm) thick, and cut two 3/16 in (5 mm) lengths for the arms. Roll each into a ball and then form it into a short log with one end more pointed. Brush the top of the body with water and press on the arms, pointed ends upward.

4 Form a 1/4 in (6 mm) ball of clay for the head and press it onto the wetted top of the body, covering the tops of the arms. Press a large yarn needle horizontally across the front of the face to indent it.

5 Cut thin slices from the 1/16 in (1.5 mm) thick log for ears. Brush the top of the head with water and press the slices onto the top of the head, 1/16 in (1.5 mm) apart.

6 Use a fine yarn needle to push a hole into each ear, pressing the ear onto the head at the same time to secure it.

7 Use the fine needle to make two eye holes in the indented part of the face. Cut a tiny chip of clay and use a knife to press it onto the bottom of the indented part for the nose, using a dab of water to make it stick.

8 Push a peg and loop finding into the top back of the head for hanging the charm. Dry the teddy and sand any rough areas. Fire and then brush. Either leave the silver brushed for a satin finish or burnish for a shine.

CHILDREN'S CHARMS

Baby rattles

This project shows how you can use silver clay to make components for charms and then complete the charms with purchased parts. The rattle's handle is made in silver clay and then a metal or glass bead is used for the head of the rattle. If you would prefer to make your own bead, follow the instructions for gemstone beads on page 110, but make the bead hole smaller.

Tools and materials

- Basic toolkit (see page 124)
- Silver clay: 5 g for rolling out (each rattle uses 1 g)
- Round cutters: ¹⁄₈ in (3 mm) and ³⁄₁₆ in (5 mm)
- Pure silver wire: 1 in (25 mm) length of 20 gauge (0.8 mm) wire
- Metal or glass bead: ⁵⁄₁₆ in (8 mm)

1 Roll out a sheet of clay, 4 p.c. (1 mm) thick, and use a straight blade to cut a ¹⁄₃₂ in (1 mm) wide strip. Press one end of the strip onto a ceramic tile to secure it and then twist the other end to make a twisted rod. Press the other end of the rod down to prevent unwinding.

2 From the same sheet of clay, cut a circle with the larger round cutter and then cut the center of the circle with the smaller cutter to make a ring. Remove the waste clay from around the outside. Allow to air dry for a few minutes, then pierce the inner circle with a darning needle held at a shallow angle and lift it clear.

DIMENSIONS

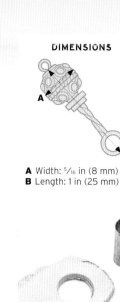

A Width: 5/16 in (8 mm)
B Length: 1 in (25 mm)

ACTUAL SIZE

BABY RATTLES

Glass bead *Try using different colored glass beads instead of metal beads.*

Rattling rattle *To make a rattle head that rattles, insert a tiny bead into a large hollow metal bead before attaching it to the wire. The wire will fill the bead hole sufficiently to trap the tiny bead inside.*

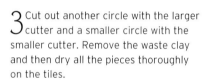

3 Cut out another circle with the larger cutter and a smaller circle with the smaller cutter. Remove the waste clay and then dry all the pieces thoroughly on the tiles.

4 Use a craft knife to cut a 1/4 in (6 mm) length from the center of the twisted rod (to avoid the pressed down ends). Apply paste to one end of the rod, press it against the side of the ring to form the rattle's handle, and then dry.

5 Apply paste to the top of the larger circle, press it onto the smaller circle, and then dry. Use a 1 mm drill bit to drill a hole in the center of the larger circle (this is for the silver wire that will hold the bead that forms the head of the rattle).

6 Apply a large blob of paste to the top of the smaller circle. Press on the unattached end of the twisted rod, holding it as vertical as you can until it sets, then dry thoroughly.

7 Apply paste to the end of the silver wire and insert it into the drilled hole. Dry the piece again, then sand or file any rough edges carefully. Fire and polish. Oxidize if you want an antique look.

8 Thread the bead onto the silver wire and trim the wire to 1/4 in (6 mm) from the bead. Use round-nose pliers to turn a loop in the end of the wire. You can attach the jump ring through this loop or through the handle ring, as you prefer.

Ducklings

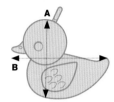

DIMENSIONS

A Height: ½ in (13 mm)
B Width: ⅝ in (15 mm)

ACTUAL SIZE

Ducklings are popular motifs for children—they decorate children's fabrics, they feature in children's picture books, and they are made into a variety of toys both for the bath and to pull along. Ducklings therefore make appealing silver charms to decorate a child's bracelet, as a tiny pendant for a little girl, or as a fun pair of dangling earrings for the young at heart.

1 Form a ⁵⁄₁₆ in (8 mm) ball of clay and roll one side between your fingers to shape it into a teardrop for the duckling's body.

2 Press the body down onto a moistened ceramic tile to stick it in place—it is easier to work on the clay if it is attached to a work surface. Use a craft knife to push up the pointed end to form the duckling's tail.

PROJECT 20
SKILL LEVEL ★

DUCKLINGS

Tools and materials

- Basic toolkit (see page 124)
- Silver clay: 3 g per duckling
- Teardrop cutter: ³/₁₆ in (5 mm)
- Peg and loop finding

Bead eyes To add sparkle to the duckling, press a size 15/0 (1.5 mm) fireable glass seed bead into each eye hole before drying and firing.

Added wings Instead of indented wings, create a more three-dimensional effect by forming two tiny teardrops of clay and flattening them between your fingers for wings. Use water or paste to attach one on each side of the body, curved upward at the back. Mark feathers as for the indented wings.

3 To suggest wings, impress both sides of the body with a teardrop cutter, with the pointed end toward the duckling's tail.

4 Use the eye of a darning needle to mark feathers on the front half of each wing.

5 Form a ¼ in (6 mm) ball of clay for the head. Brush the top front of the body with water and then press the ball down onto the body to make a firm join.

6 Roll a log of clay, ¹/₁₆ in (1.5 mm) thick and pointed at one end. Cut off the pointed end for the beak, about ¹/₁₆ in (1.5 mm) from the end of the log.

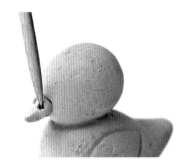

7 Brush the front of the head with water and then press the cut end of the beak onto the head, just below the midway point. Curve the beak up slightly and use the pointed end of the darning needle to make two nostril holes in the top of the beak, pushing the beak toward the head with the needle as you make each hole.

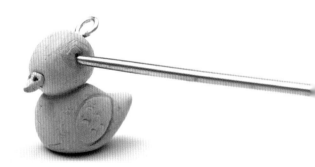

8 Push a peg and loop finding firmly into the top of the head. Make two holes for eyes with a fine yarn needle. Dry, sand if required to smooth, then fire and polish.

Ballet

A dainty pair of ballet shoes complete with silver ribbons makes the perfect gift for a ballet enthusiast. Sculpting the shoes is not difficult, but the ribbon is more challenging. Make sure that the ribbon clay is well hydrated. If you find the ribbon difficult in silver clay, make it in pale pink or white polymer clay, which is easier to handle.

Tools and materials

- Basic toolkit (see page 124)
- Silver clay: 5 g for rolling out (each ballet shoes charm uses about 2.5 g)
- Paintbrush handle for forming: about $1/8$ in (3 mm) thick with a rounded end

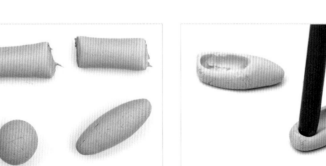

1 Form a $3/16$ in (5 mm) thick log of silver clay and cut two $3/8$ in (10 mm) lengths for the shoes. Roll each length into a ball, and then roll each ball into a log with rounded ends.

2 Press the end of a paintbrush handle into the center of one of the logs and continue pressing toward the heel of the shoe to hollow it out. With the handle still in the shoe, press a finger against the heel to shape it. Repeat for the other shoe.

3 Brush water onto one of the shoes and press the other shoe on top at an angle.

BALLET

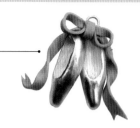

Colored ribbons Make the ballet shoes in silver clay but do not make the ribbons. Pierce with a peg and loop finding in the heel, then fire and polish. Make the ribbon streamers using pastel-colored polymer clay. Press onto the shoes and arrange the ribbons, then bake the whole piece as recommended on the package of polymer clay. Use epoxy or superglue to attach the polymer clay bow to the silver shoes when cool.

DIMENSIONS

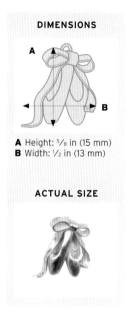

A Height: ⁵⁄₈ in (15 mm)
B Width: ¹⁄₂ in (13 mm)

ACTUAL SIZE

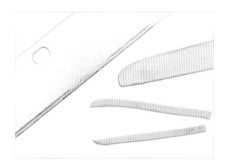

4 To make the ribbon, roll out a sheet of clay, 1 p.c. (0.25 mm) thick. Smear the clay with oil to prevent the blade from sticking and use a straight blade to cut two strips, ¹⁄₁₆ in (1.5 mm) wide and ³⁄₄ in (20 mm) long.

5 Cut one end of each ribbon strip at an angle. Apply paste to the top of the heel of the upper shoe and press the straight ends of the two ribbons on top, angling the ribbons out over the shoes and curling them slightly into a graceful curve for the bow streamers.

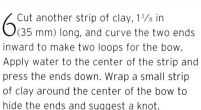

6 Cut another strip of clay, 1³⁄₈ in (35 mm) long, and curve the two ends inward to make two loops for the bow. Apply water to the center of the strip and press the ends down. Wrap a small strip of clay around the center of the bow to hide the ends and suggest a knot.

7 Apply paste to the top of the ribbon streamers and press on the bow, arranging it to drape attractively.

8 Push a peg and loop finding into the heel of the top shoe, just behind the bow. Dry the shoes, fill any cracks with paste, and smooth carefully. The ribbons will be fragile until fired. Fire, brush, and polish. File any sharp points on the ribbon ends.

Music

These silver charms are the perfect gift for musical people. Creating a miniature musical instrument would be challenging, but these musical notes and symbol charms are much easier to make. They are also suitable for all types of music enthusiasts, whatever their instrument or musical tastes. Hydrate the clay well to give yourself maximum working time.

TEMPLATES

Templates are shown actual size. Extend the guidelines so that you can see them when the clay is placed on top.

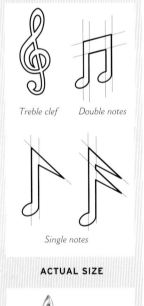

Treble clef   Double notes

Single notes

ACTUAL SIZE

Tools and materials

- Basic toolkit (see page 124)
- Silver clay: 3 g for rolling out (each music charm uses 1 g or less)
- Template: traced or photocopied and taped to a ceramic tile
- Piece of clear acetate or plastic cut from a window carton taped over the template
- Wet wipe

TREBLE CLEF

1 Roll a long thin log of clay, about $\frac{1}{32}$ in (1 mm) thick and 3 in (7.5 cm) long. Use a log roller to help you roll it thinly and evenly.

2 Roll one end of the log into a point. Wipe over the acetate with a wet wipe to moisten the surface lightly and help the clay to stick. Curve the log around the bottom curve and up to the top of the line.

3 Trim the top at an angle. Form a point at the end of the remaining log as before. Brush water over the first clay shape to help the next piece to stick. Coil the log over the first piece, following the template up to the top. Trim the top at an angle.

Single notes These are made in the same way as the other motifs, using the templates provided. Cut the flags straight as shown in each template and then, while the clay is still soft, curve them slightly downward to finish the note.

4 Pinch the two trimmed ends at the top together with a dab of water to hold them—a pair of yarn needles is useful for pushing the ends together neatly. Brush a dab of paste onto the bottom curl of the motif and press on a small ball of clay to finish the curl.

5 Allow the piece to dry on the acetate overnight (added heat would buckle the acetate), then remove the acetate and dry the clay fully. Fire and polish. The charm can be hung by attaching a jump ring through the top loop.

DOUBLE NOTES

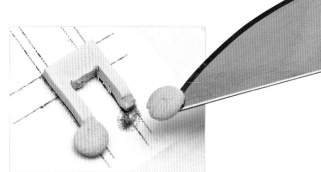

6 Prepare the template and acetate as before. Roll out the clay, 4 p.c. (1 mm) thick, and use a straight blade to cut one side straight. Lay the clay sheet on the acetate so that the straight edge is along the far left vertical guideline.

7 Use a craft knife to cut out the shape of the note stems and top bar all in one piece, following the guidelines on the template. Press the bottom of each stem to thin it slightly.

8 Brush water onto the bottom of each stem, then apply two small oval balls of clay for the note heads. Mark a pilot hole in the top bar with a fine yarn needle, then dry overnight on the acetate. File any rough edges, drill the hanging hole with a 1 mm bit, then fire and polish.

Books

These tiny books really open and have paper pages and silver covers. The pages inside the books can be left blank, or they could contain tiny messages or good wishes. Take care not to get these little charms wet or the paper will be ruined.

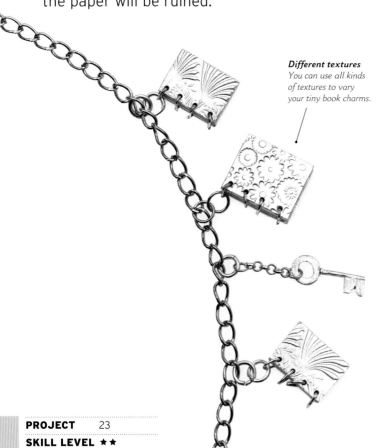

Different textures
You can use all kinds of textures to vary your tiny book charms.

Tools and materials

- Basic toolkit (see page 124)
- Silver clay: 7 g for rolling out (each book uses about 4 g)
- Texture sheet or rubber stamp
- Template: ⅝ x 1 in (15 x 25 mm) rectangle of paper with a line drawn down the center parallel to the shorter edges
- Thin paper for the pages of the book (copier paper is fine)
- Sharp scissors
- Scrap thick cardstock
- Needle tool: a sharp needle held in a wooden handle for punching holes in the paper
- Sterling silver or silver-plated wire: four 1 in (25 mm) lengths of 20 gauge (0.8 mm) wire

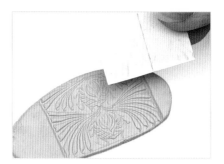

1 To make the book covers, roll out a sheet of clay, 4 p.c. (1 mm), thick, and texture one side using a texture sheet (see page 20, steps 2–3) or rubber stamp (see page 36, steps 1–2). Place the clay on a ceramic tile and lay the template on top.

2 Use a straight blade to cut the clay sheet around the outside of the template, aligning symmetrical patterns if necessary. Cut the rectangular piece of clay exactly in half, using the template to guide you.

BOOKS

DIMENSIONS	ACTUAL SIZE

A Height: 5/8 in (15 mm)
B Width: 1/2 in (13 mm)

Picture books *Try using paper printed with text or pictures inside the book instead of plain paper.*

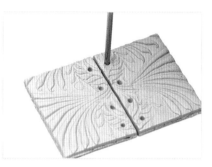

3 Use a fine yarn needle to mark four evenly spaced holes along each side of the center cut, aligning the holes on each side. The end holes should be 1/16 in (1.5 mm) in from the edge and all the holes should be this distance from the center cut.

4 Dry the book covers on the tile and then sand the edges if required to smooth them. Use a 1 mm drill bit to drill the holes. Fire the book covers and then brush and burnish.

5 To make the pages of the book, cut a 3/4 x 4 in (20 x 100 mm) strip of paper. Fold in half and then in half twice more to make a 3/4 x 1/2 in (20 x 13 mm) rectangle that is eight sheets thick. Trim around the outside of the sheets with sharp scissors, just in from the folded edges, to make a stack of tiny pages.

6 Assemble the pages between the two covers, trimming them further if necessary. Holding the components together, tap the spine edge of the book (the side with the holes) on a work surface to make the pages level with the edges of the covers on that side.

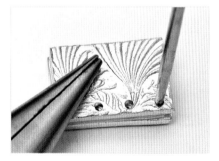

7 Place the book on a piece of thick cardstock. Pierce firmly with a needle tool into each hole to punch through the stack of pages inside. Thread a length of silver wire through each of the four sets of holes and bend the wire around to cross over the spine of the book.

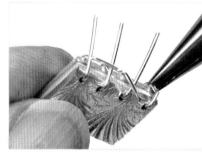

8 Using wire cutters, trim both ends of each crossed wire. Use fine-nose pliers to bend the cut ends together to form four closed binding rings. Adjust the rings so that the book opens and closes freely. Hang the charm by attaching a jump ring through the top binding ring.

Tools and materials

- Basic toolkit (see page 124)
- Silver clay syringe with medium (1 mm) nozzle: about 2 g of clay per charm
- Toilet tissue paper: about ¼ sheet of 2-ply paper, depending on the thickness
- Scrap of polymer clay or small jelly jar
- Peg and loop finding
- Sterling silver headpins: two 1 in (25 mm) long pins
- Epoxy glue or superglue

Knitting

Knitting has surged in popularity in recent years, and this little charm is an ideal gift for any knitting enthusiast. This project uses a syringe to pipe the fine lines of the yarn. Work in small sections rather than try to pipe the yarn in a continuous line. Simply dab down onto the piece with the tip of the syringe to start or end a line of clay. To save silver, the yarn is built over a ball of toilet tissue paper that burns away during firing.

Ball band *Shape the toilet paper into a long ball with a waist. Syringe over the paper as before, avoiding the waist part. Wrap a label made from a lightly textured thin sheet of clay around the center of the ball.*

Fine colored yarn *Use a fine (0.5 mm) nozzle on the syringe to pipe finer yarn. Paint the yarn ball in a bright color using glass paint.*

1 Form the toilet paper into a rough ball, then wet it and squeeze out excess moisture. Roll it into a ball, about ³/₈ in (10 mm) diameter. Make a hole in the top to take the peg and loop finding later. Allow to dry overnight or place in an oven at 300°F (150°C) for 20 minutes.

2 Pierce the bottom of the tissue ball with a darning needle to give you a handle. Using the syringe, pipe lines of clay all around the ball, letting the lines drop into place as you extrude while twirling the ball on the needle.

3 Continue building up layers until most of the paper is covered. Leave a few small spaces with the paper visible at the top and bottom of the ball for inserting the knitting needles and finding later.

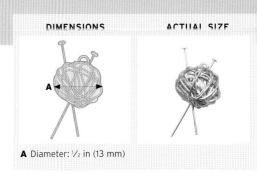

A Diameter: 1/2 in (13 mm)

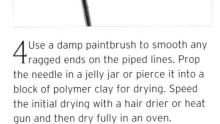

4 Use a damp paintbrush to smooth any ragged ends on the piped lines. Prop the needle in a jelly jar or pierce it into a block of polymer clay for drying. Speed the initial drying with a hair drier or heat gun and then dry fully in an oven.

5 Push the peg of the finding into the hole made earlier in the top of the ball. Pipe more lines of clay around the loop to make sure that it is secured on all sides in the clay. Dry again thoroughly.

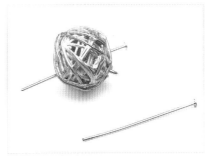

6 If using a gas burner or torch, fire the ball with a low flame. The paper will ignite and flame up. After it has burnt away, fire fully for the usual time. If using a kiln, fire at 1200°F (650°C) for 20 minutes, then at the full temperature and time recommended for the type of clay.

7 Cool and brush the piece, then burnish lightly over the threads of silver. Use a file to sharpen the ends of the headpins into a slight point. Do not make them too pointed or they will catch on clothing.

8 Push the headpins through the ball of yarn at an angle. Ease open any gaps that are too small, or use a fine drill bit in a pin vise. Secure the pins in place with a drop of epoxy or superglue.

Color *Use glass paints to paint the cars in bright colors.*

Tools and materials

- Basic toolkit (see page 124)
- Silver clay: 3 g per car
- Peg and loop finding
- Drill bits: 1 mm and 1.5 mm

Cars

Cute little cars to whiz around your wrist—what car enthusiast could resist these charms? The shape is very simple and requires minimal modeling. The wheels are added after drying so that they look neat and round.

1 Form a ³⁄₈ in (10 mm) ball of clay and shape it into an oval. Press it down onto a ceramic tile and pinch it into a roughly rectangular shape. Press the blade of a craft knife down onto the front third of the clay to form the car hood.

2 Make the windshield by angling the knife blade up from the hood toward the roof of the car and pressing.

3 Use the tip of a fine yarn needle to mark details on the clay surface—the windshield, the side and back windows, and lines to suggest the doors.

CARS

Convertible Make a convertible by adding the chassis in two separate pieces on top of a small rectangle cut from a sheet of clay.

Car designs Alter the shape of the car by making the hood longer or by modeling the trunk to suggest different makes of car.

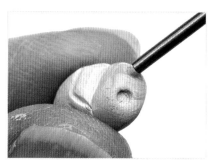

4 Press the flat end of a 1.5 mm drill bit into the clay at the front of the car to form the headlamps.

5 Roll a ¹⁄₁₆ in (1.5 mm) thick log of clay and cut four ¹⁄₁₆ in (1.5 mm) lengths from it. Roll each length into a ball and press down onto a tile to make ⅛ in (3 mm) diameter disks for the car wheels. Press the center of each wheel with the flat end of the 1.5 mm drill bit for hubcaps. Dry the wheels on the tile.

6 Use paste to attach the wheels to the sides of the car, making sure that the wheels are straight and that they protrude just below the bottom of the car. Dry thoroughly.

7 Use a 1 mm drill bit to drill a hole in the roof at the rear of the car and use paste to insert a peg and loop finding. Dry again, then fire and brush.

8 Burnish the windows of the car to make them shiny, leaving the rest of the car matte silver.

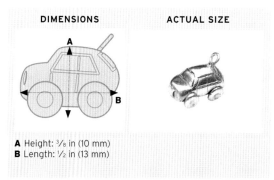

DIMENSIONS   ACTUAL SIZE

A Height: ⅜ in (10 mm)
B Length: ½ in (13 mm)

Tools and materials

- Basic toolkit (see page 124)
- Silver clay: 5 g for rolling out (each boat uses 2 g)
- Templates: traced or photocopied and cut out
- Peg and loop finding
- Silver clay syringe with medium (1 mm) nozzle
- Paper tissue

Sailing

This tiny sailing yacht is relatively challenging and requires repeated drying of the parts as you create the boat. The difficult part is attaching the dried sails to the hull; to make this easier, you could sand the bottom of the hull flat so that the boat stands up while you work on it. Careful syringing is required to apply delicate details as well as reinforcement.

1 Form a ¼ in (6 mm) ball of clay and roll it into a log, ¾ in (20 mm) long and pointed at both ends. Press the log lightly down onto a ceramic tile and pinch along the top to shape the bottom of the boat's hull.

2 Shape the stern (back) of the hull by cutting off one end, angling the knife blade outward. Dry the hull, then sand to smooth and refine the shape.

DIMENSIONS

A Height: ⅞ in (22 mm)
B Width: ¾ in (20 mm)

ACTUAL SIZE

TEMPLATES
Templates are shown actual size.

Front sail   *Back sail*

PROJECT 26
SKILL LEVEL ★★★

SAILING

Colored hull Paint the hull of the boat with glass paint in a bright color.

Flags Roll out a sheet of clay, 2 p.c. (0.5 mm) thick. Cut out a small rectangle and curve it over needles to dry. Roll a thin log of clay for the pole, add a small ball to the top, and dry. Paste the dried flag to the pole and attach a peg and loop finding with paste. Use glass paints to color the flag.

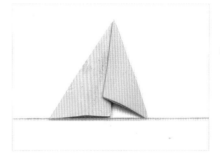

Sails The sails hide the mast on one side of the charm.

3 Roll out a sheet of clay, 2 p.c. (0.5 mm) thick. Lay on the templates and cut out the sails using a straight blade.

4 With the sails oriented as shown, shape each sail into a gentle curve over a large yarn needle placed vertically under it. Dry the pieces on the needles.

5 Lay the dried large sail on a tile with the bottom against the edge of a rolling guide to keep it straight. Apply paste along the vertical edge and press the small sail on top at a slight angle, with the bottom point touching the rolling guide to align the sails. Dry the pieces.

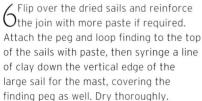

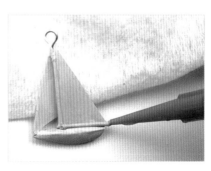

6 Flip over the dried sails and reinforce the join with more paste if required. Attach the peg and loop finding to the top of the sails with paste, then syringe a line of clay down the vertical edge of the large sail for the mast, covering the finding peg as well. Dry thoroughly.

7 Apply paste generously to the top of the hull and push the bottom of the sails onto it, with the small sail to the front and both sails fully vertical. Hold for a few minutes until the paste sets and then dry thoroughly, propping with a paper tissue for support.

8 Syringe a line of clay along the base of the large sail to reinforce the join and suggest the boom of the sail. Syringe a dab of clay at the base of the mast and bottom point of the small sail to reinforce further. Dry and fire, then polish with care to avoid breaking the delicate parts.

Tools and materials

- Basic toolkit (see page 124)
- Silver clay: 5 g for rolling out (each racket and ball uses 1.5 g)
- Polymer clay for making texture sheet
- Talcum powder
- Fine sieve or tea strainer with wire or nylon mesh
- Round cutter: ³⁄₈ in (10 mm)
- Peg and loop finding

Tennis

These tiny tennis racket charms for the budding tennis ace are fairly easy to make using a homemade texture sheet for the racket strings. If you do not have a fine tea strainer or sieve for texturing the polymer clay, you can use a piece of fine-grained cotton fabric instead.

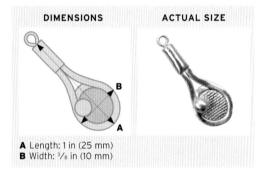

DIMENSIONS	ACTUAL SIZE

A Length: 1 in (25 mm)
B Width: ³⁄₈ in (10 mm)

1 Roll out the polymer clay, 4 p.c. (1 mm) thick, and cut out two 2 in (50 mm) squares. Dust them with talcum powder to prevent sticking and press each powdered side firmly onto the sieve to take an impression. Bake the clay as recommended on the package.

2 Roll out a sheet of silver clay, 2 p.c. (0.5 mm) thick and larger than the round cutter. Lightly oil both surfaces and sandwich between the two polymer clay texture sheets. Press firmly to make an impression on both sides of the silver sheet.

3 Smooth the textured silver clay onto a ceramic tile and cut out a circle with the cutter. Use the cutter to trim the sides of the circle to make an oval.

TENNIS

Hanging position
Attach the peg and loop finding to the head of the racket for a different hang.

Bead and chain Use a round bead as a tennis ball. Thread the bead onto a headpin, attach the pin to a fine silver chain, and connect the other end of the chain to the jump ring that hangs the racket.

4 Roll out a sheet of silver clay, 4 p.c. (1 mm) thick. Use a straight blade to cut a 1/16 x 2 in (1.5 x 50 mm) strip. Brush water on the bottom edge of the oval and push a 1/2 in (13 mm) length of the strip against it, curving it around. Trim to shape as shown.

5 Brush water around the top and side edges of the oval and press the center of the remaining strip onto the top, curving it around and down the sides and pushing it against the oval to secure.

6 Push the ends of the strip together and trim to 1/4 in (6 mm) from the bottom of the racket head.

7 Roll a log of silver clay, 1/8 in (3 mm) thick, and cut a 1/4 in (6 mm) length. Brush paste on one cut end and press it against the trimmed strips of the racket to form the handle.

8 Push a peg and loop finding into the end of the handle. Roll an 1/8 in (3 mm) ball of silver clay for the tennis ball and attach it to the racket strings with paste. Dry and fire.

FASHION CHARMS

High-heeled shoes

Dainty stiletto heels make appealing charms, and you can have fun thinking of different decorations for the toes of the shoes. Although these charms are tiny and intricate-looking, they are not difficult to make.

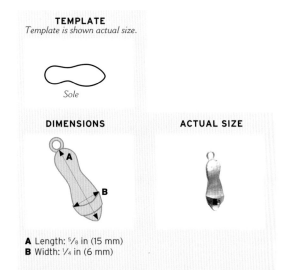

TEMPLATE
Template is shown actual size.

Sole

DIMENSIONS

A Length: 5/8 in (15 mm)
B Width: 1/4 in (6 mm)

ACTUAL SIZE

1 Roll out a sheet of clay, 2 p.c. (0.5 mm) thick. Smooth it onto a ceramic tile and lay the template for the shoe sole on top. Use a fine sharp needle held vertically to cut around the template, then remove the waste clay.

2 Slide a blade under the sole to free it from the tile. Place the handle of a modeling tool or paintbrush on the tile. Press the toe of the sole onto the tile and lift the heel onto the handle so that it is supported in a raised curve. Dry the piece on the handle.

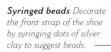

Syringed beads Decorate the front strap of the shoe by syringing dots of silver clay to suggest beads.

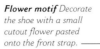

Flower motif Decorate the shoe with a small cutout flower pasted onto the front strap.

Strappy sandal Use two or more thin strips for the front of the shoe.

3 Form a ³⁄₁₆ in (5 mm) ball of clay and point one end to make a teardrop. Roll the pointed end between your forefingers to thin it into a drumstick shape.

4 Lay the drumstick on a tile and cut off the thick end at an angle. Trim the thin end so that the heel is ³⁄₁₆ in (5 mm) long.

5 Roll out a small sheet of clay, 2 p.c. (0.5 mm) thick, and cut an ¹⁄₈ x ³⁄₈ in (3 x 10 mm) strip. Brush paste on each side of the sole front. Press the ends of the strip onto the pasted sides, curving the strip up in the middle and trimming if necessary.

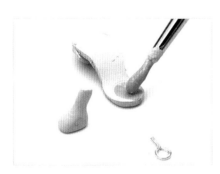

6 Dry all the pieces. Apply a generous blob of paste to the underside of the sole heel. Press the peg of the finding onto the paste.

7 Apply paste to the top of the heel and press this over the finding. Brush on more paste to cover any gaps or cracks and then dry.

8 Use a fine file to correct any rough parts. File the bottom of the heel so that the shoe stands upright. Fire the shoe, then brush and polish.

Purses

A woman's purse is her world on the move, so what better symbol for a charm? This simple project uses rolled out clay in much the same way as making a bag from leather or fabric. Work with well-hydrated clay and have fun decorating this little purse, from texturing the clay to adding straps, chains, or clasps.

Tools and materials

- Basic toolkit (see page 124)
- Silver clay: 5 g for rolling out (each purse uses 2 g)
- Heart cutter: 3/16 in (5 mm)

DIMENSIONS

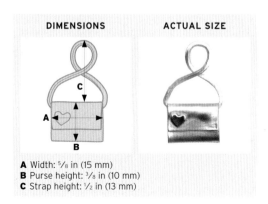

ACTUAL SIZE

A Width: 5/8 in (15 mm)
B Purse height: 3/8 in (10 mm)
C Strap height: 1/2 in (13 mm)

1 Roll out a sheet of clay, 2 p.c. (0.5 mm) thick, and use a straight blade to cut a 5/8 x 1 1/8 in (15 x 30 mm) rectangle. Mark light guidelines on the rectangle to divide it into thirds for the front, back, and flap of the purse.

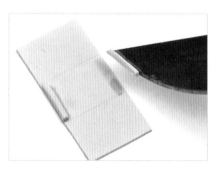

2 Roll out a small sheet of clay, 4 p.c. (1 mm) thick, and cut two 1/16 x 3/8 in (1.5 x 10 mm) strips. Brush water on the sides of the middle section of the purse and press a strip on each side.

PURSES

Purse with catch Make a catch for the purse by pressing a tiny strip of clay over the center front edge of the flap.

Evening purse Texture the clay with lace fabric. When folding over the flap, paste a peg and loop finding into the top of the purse on each side. Fire and polish, then attach a small length of chain for hanging.

3 Cut a small piece of clay from the same sheet to fit in the space between the two applied strips. Brush water on the space between the strips and press on the small piece. This will plump out the purse without using too much clay.

4 Brush water on the strips and fold up the lower section of the purse, pressing it down lightly to form the main pocket of the purse.

5 Apply paste along the top edge of the pocket and then fold down the top section to form the flap, pressing to secure. The edge of the flap should be about 1/8 in (3 mm) above the bottom of the purse.

6 Cut a 1/16 x 2 in (1.5 x 50 mm) strip from a 2 p.c. (0.5 mm) thick sheet of clay. Paste one end into the top of the purse for the strap. Curve it into a loop for hanging, trim if necessary, and paste the other end into the other side of the purse.

7 Cut out a tiny heart from a 1 p.c. (0.25 mm) thick sheet of clay and paste it onto the front flap as decoration.

8 Brush paste into the sides of the purse to cover the joins. Dry, sand any rough areas, and fire.

Dresses

Dress charms are fun to make yourself because you can decorate the basic shape to create a charm that is a miniature version of a real dress. These tiny and detailed charms are very fragile in the plaster-dry stage, so take care when sanding and drilling the hole.

Tools and materials

- Basic toolkit (see page 124)
- Silver clay: 3 g for rolling out (each dress uses 1 g or less)

DIMENSIONS

A Height: ³/₄ in (20 mm)
B Width: ⁵/₈ in (15 mm)

ACTUAL SIZE

1 Roll out a sheet of clay, 4 p.c. (1 mm) thick, and cut a ¹/₄ x ³/₄ in (6 x 20 mm) strip. Lay the strip on a ceramic tile and cut out two rectangles to leave a hanger shape, with arms about ¹/₁₆ in (1.5 mm) wide and a small rectangle in the center.

2 Pull down the ends of the two arms to make a curved hanger shape. Trim around the top of the small rectangle to round it and pierce with a fine yarn needle for drilling later.

DRESSES

Cocktail dress Cut out a simple dress shape from a sheet of clay and attach to the hanger with the dress shoulders curved over the hanger.

Sash dress Cut wider straps and add a strip of clay as a sash. Mark details along the sash and bottom of the skirt with the eye of a fine needle to suggest frills.

3 Roll out a sheet of clay, 2 p.c. (0.5 mm) thick, and cut two $\frac{1}{32}$ x $\frac{1}{2}$ in (1 x 13 mm) strips for the dress straps. Brush water over the arms of the hanger and apply the strips, curving them over at the top.

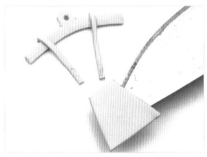

4 From the same sheet of clay, cut out a $\frac{1}{2}$ in (13 mm) square. Trim the two sides at an angle to make a skirt shape. Wet the bottom of the straps and press the top of the skirt over them, leaving a $\frac{1}{4}$ in (6 mm) gap between the skirt and the hanger.

5 Trim the bottom edge of the skirt into a slight curve. Mark vertical lines with a fine yarn needle to suggest folds, then push the tip of the needle against the bottom edge of the skirt to scallop it on the folds.

6 Form two scant $\frac{1}{8}$ in (3 mm) balls of clay. Brush water over the top of the skirt and lower straps, then press a ball down on each side for the bodice, covering the bottom of the straps and the top of the skirt.

7 Use a wet paintbrush and paste to smooth the balls of clay together to form the bodice.

8 Dry the dress on the tile. Use paste to reinforce and smooth the back where the straps join the skirt and over the top of the hanger. Dry again. Drill the hole in the hanger using a 1 mm bit. Sand any rough areas, then fire and polish.

Hats

Summer hats Use glass paints to color ribbons, flowers, and leaves in bright colors to look like summery straw hats. Protect the color with varnish.

Tools and materials

- Basic toolkit (see page 124)
- Silver clay: 5 g for rolling out (each hat uses 2 g)
- Small piece of polymer clay to make a hat form
- Round cutter: ³⁄₄ in (20 mm)
- Polymer clay texture sheet made from fine sieve (see page 72, step 1)
- Leaf and flower cutters: ³⁄₁₆ in (5 mm)

A pretty hat has timeless appeal and these little silver charms could be from virtually any period, from the Victorian era to the present day. A homemade texture sheet gives the effect of woven straw. Work with well-hydrated clay and decorate the hat with ribbons or flowers as you wish.

1 To make a hat form, shape a ³⁄₁₆ in (5 mm) ball of polymer clay and press it down onto a ceramic tile until it is firmly attached and slightly flattened. Press the blade of a craft knife against the sides to straighten them.

2 Roll out a sheet of silver clay, 2 p.c. (0.5 mm) thick, and cut out a circle with a round cutter. Smear with oil. Press oiled side down onto the texture sheet, taking care not to distort the round shape but pressing the edges to thin them.

3 Place the textured circle centrally over the hat form, pressing it down over the form to shape the crown of the hat. Use a large yarn needle to press in the sides. Press the texture sheet over the top of the crown if necessary to re-texture it.

HATS

DIMENSIONS

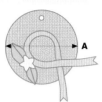

A Diameter: ³/₄ in (20 mm)

ACTUAL SIZE

Rose and streamers Attach a tiny rose (see page 38) to the leaves instead of a cutout flower. Make the ribbon streamers longer and shape into waves before drying.

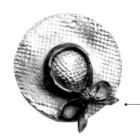

Hat with bow Make a bow and attach it to the crossed ribbon (see page 61, step 6).

4 Use the needle to lift the brim of the hat in several places to make the brim wavy. Support the curves with a tool or needle to hold them until they are dry. For a more formal hat, leave the brim straight.

5 Roll out a sheet of silver clay, 2 p.c. (0.5 mm) thick, and cut a ¹/₁₆ x 2 in (1.5 x 50 mm) strip. Brush water along the strip and press it around the crown of the hat for a ribbon. Overlap the ends and trim each end into a double point just beyond the brim.

6 Use a fine yarn needle to mark a pilot hole in the brim for hanging. Using cutters, cut out two leaves and a flower from the 2 p.c. (0.5 mm) thick clay. Paste the leaves onto the brim. Press the needle onto each flower petal to cup it.

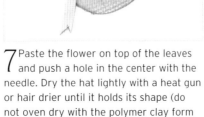

7 Paste the flower on top of the leaves and push a hole in the center with the needle. Dry the hat lightly with a heat gun or hair drier until it holds its shape (do not oven dry with the polymer clay form inside or it will burn).

8 Remove the polymer clay form, then dry the hat fully in an oven. Drill the hanging hole with a 1 mm bit and sand to remove any blemishes. Fire and polish, or leave the hat brushed silver and burnish the ribbon for contrast.

Parasols

Parasols and umbrellas are always popular designs for charms and for good reason—they symbolize protection; they come in lots of gorgeous colors; and they can be plain and serviceable or frilly and feminine. These little charms use a marble as a form to create the basic shape; then after firing, the wire handle is crimped in place.

Bead handle *Thread colored beads onto a 1 in (25 mm) headpin and crimp in place. Thread on a second crimp and then the canopy, and turn a loop in the end of the headpin. Secure the canopy in place on the headpin using the second crimp.*

1 Roll out a sheet of clay, 2 p.c. (0.5 mm) thick, and cut out a circle with the round cutter. Stand the cutter on a ceramic tile, prop the marble in the cutter, and smooth the clay circle onto the marble to form the canopy of the parasol.

DIMENSIONS

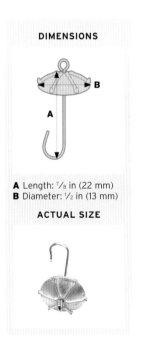

A Length: ⁷/₈ in (22 mm)
B Diameter: ¹/₂ in (13 mm)

ACTUAL SIZE

Tools and materials

- Basic toolkit (see page 124)
- Silver clay: 5 g for rolling out (each parasol uses 1 g)
- Round cutter: ¹/₂ in (13 mm)
- Standard glass marble: ⁵/₈ in (15 mm)
- Silver clay syringe with medium (1 mm) nozzle
- Sterling silver wire: 1 ¹/₂ in (40 mm) length of 20 gauge (0.8 mm) wire
- Silver tube or bead crimp: 1.5 mm

Beaded edge *Syringe a line of clay dots all around the edge of the canopy.*

2 Use a yarn needle to mark a hole in the center of the circle as a guide. Make tiny marks evenly spaced around the edge of the circle as a guide for the ribs—eight or six ribs is the usual number.

3 Syringe ribs of clay from the center out to the edge. Start by dabbing down just outside the central hole, then syringe each line to the edge, and finish with another dab to cut the thread of clay.

4 Dry the clay on the marble (it can go in an oven without harm, but cool it slowly to avoid cracking). Sand away any blemishes and drill the central hole with a 1 mm drill bit. Fire the canopy, then brush and polish.

5 Use round-nose pliers to turn a loop at one end of the silver wire. Thread the other end through the canopy until the loop lies against the top. Thread the crimp onto the long end of the wire.

Colored umbrella *Instead of syringing the ribs, cut thin strips from a sheet of clay. Use a round cutter to cut out scallops of clay between the ribs. Paint the sections of the canopy with different colored glass paints.*

6 Push the crimp up against the underside of the canopy. Holding it tight against the canopy, squeeze crimp with pliers to fix it onto the wire and hold the canopy firmly in place.

7 Use round-nose pliers to turn the end of the wire into a large curve for the handle. Bend the end of the wire out a little to form a shepherd's crook shape.

Dogs

Dogs come in all shapes and sizes. Templates are provided for four popular breeds, but you could use a profile photograph of your own pet to create a silhouette instead (see page 100). It is easier to cut out an intricate shape in thinner clay, but you can make the clay thicker if you prefer. The hanging loop is cut out of the clay sheet as an integral part of the charm.

TEMPLATES
Templates are shown actual size.

Scottie

Labrador

Yorkshire Terrier

Dachshund

ACTUAL SIZE

Tools and materials
- Basic toolkit (see page 124)
- Silver clay: 5 g for rolling out (each dog uses 1 g or less)
- Template: traced or photocopied and cut out
- Engraving tool such as a scribe or sharp-pointed burnisher

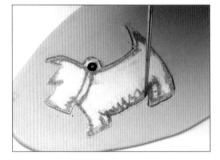

1 Roll out a sheet of clay, 2 p.c. (0.5 mm) thick. Smooth the clay onto a ceramic tile, oil the surface to help the template to stick, and lay the template on top. Use a fine sharp needle held vertically to cut around the template.

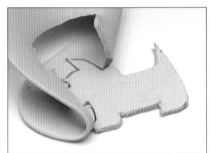

2 Wipe the needle frequently to remove any burrs of clay that build up on the needle tip. Peel away the waste clay, leaving the cutout shape on the tile. Do not attempt to move the dog shape until after drying or it will distort.

Yorkshire Terrier *While the clay is still soft, texture all over the dog with the point of a fine needle. Drag the needle off the bottom edge of the clay to suggest shaggy fur.*

Dachshund *Make sure that the hanging loop is not too far back or the dog will hang down at the front.*

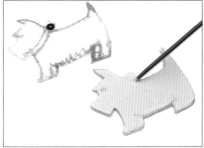

3 Use a fine yarn needle to mark details on the clay, such as the leg lines and the eye, referring to the template as a guide. Draw a line along the top of the back to define the hanging loop.

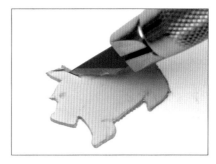

4 Use a fine knife blade or scalpel to neaten any rough edges left by the needle and make any deeper cuts. Roughen the clay edge on the stomach to suggest the ends of fur hanging down.

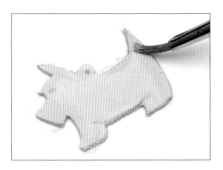

5 Brush over all the edges with a damp paintbrush to smooth them. Use the yarn needle to make a pilot hole in the hanging loop to be drilled later.

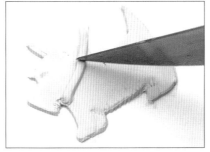

6 Cut a strip of clay for the collar and paste it into position, trimming it to fit. Dry the dog on the tile and then sand any rough areas smooth. Drill the hole for the hanging loop with a 1 mm drill bit.

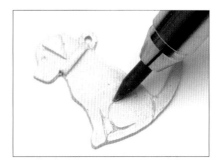

7 The Labrador and Dachshund have an applied ear, cut to shape and pasted in place. To deepen any detail lines, use an engraving tool when the clay is dry. Fire, then brush and polish, or leave with a satin finish and just burnish the collar.

Tools and materials

- Basic toolkit (see page 124)
- Silver clay: 1.5 g per cat
- Peg and loop finding

Cats

These little cat charms are fairly simple to make because they have a flat back and are sculpted on a ceramic tile. Two versions are shown here—an upright cat and a reclining cat. Always brush water onto the relevant clay surface with a fine paintbrush before pressing on added pieces of clay to make a firm bond. For such small models, using paste to secure would be messy.

DIMENSIONS

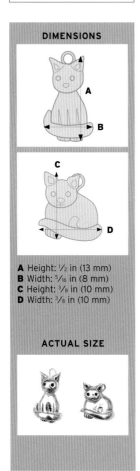

A Height: ½ in (13 mm)
B Width: ⁵⁄₁₆ in (8 mm)
C Height: ³⁄₈ in (10 mm)
D Width: ³⁄₈ in (10 mm)

ACTUAL SIZE

UPRIGHT CAT

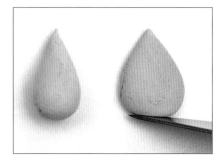

1 Form a ¼ in (6 mm) ball of clay and point one side to make a teardrop shape. Press this down onto a ceramic tile for the cat's body, then flatten the bottom with the blade of a craft knife.

2 Use the knife to mark three vertical lines on the body for the legs. Brush water onto the bottom of the cat and press on two ¹⁄₁₆ in (1.5 mm) balls of clay for the feet. Flatten the bottom of the feet with the knife blade.

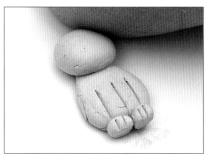

3 Use the tip of the knife blade to mark small vertical lines on the feet for the toes. Form a ³⁄₁₆ in (5 mm) ball of clay for the head. Brush water onto the top of the body and press on the head, flattening it slightly to secure.

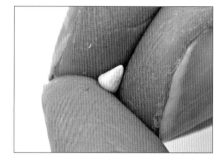

4 Form two ¹⁄₁₆ in (1.5 mm) balls of clay for the ears and pinch them between two fingers and a thumb to form triangles. Brush water onto the top of the head and press on the two ears, spaced a little apart.

5 Use a fine yarn needle to pierce ear holes and press each ear firmly onto the head with the needle in the ear hole to secure it. Mark two eyes with the needle. Cut a thin slice from a ¹⁄₃₂ in (1 mm) thick log of clay for the nose, and use the tip of the knife to apply the nose to the moistened face.

Ginger cat
Oxidize the cat to a bright orange or try to get a color similar to that of your own pet.

RECLINING CAT

6 Roll an ¹⁄₈ in (3 mm) ball of clay into a short log and point one end for the tail. Brush water onto the lower body, then press the tail in a curve across the front of the body. Push a peg and loop finding into the top of the head. Dry and fire.

7 To make a reclining cat, shape the body into an oval and press it down onto the tile in landscape orientation. Add a single foot at the bottom left and use a fine yarn needle to mark a line for the back leg. Press the head onto the top left of the body above the foot.

8 Finish the head and face as before, adding a muzzle if you wish. Mark the toes and add the tail as before. Push a peg and loop finding into the clay just behind the right ear. Dry and fire.

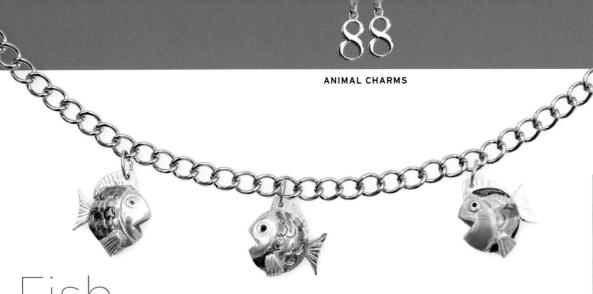

ANIMAL CHARMS

Fish

Fish are symbolic creatures in many cultures and religions. They represent fertility, happiness, and good fortune as well as transformation and creativity. This whimsical fish is made hollow for lightness and to be economical on clay.

DIMENSIONS

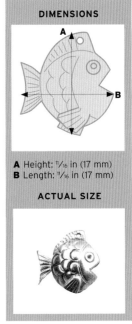

A Height: ¹¹⁄₁₆ in (17 mm)
B Length: ¹¹⁄₁₆ in (17 mm)

TEMPLATES
Templates are shown actual size.

Top fin

Tail

Side fin (cut 2)

ACTUAL SIZE

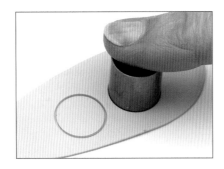

1 Roll out a sheet of clay, 2 p.c. (0.5 mm) thick, and cut out two circles using the large round cutter. These will form the two sides of the fish. Carefully peel away the waste clay.

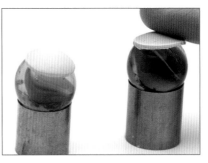

2 Stand the spare cutters onto a ceramic tile and prop a marble in each cutter (or press the marbles onto scraps of polymer clay to hold them steady). Smooth a clay circle onto each marble to form a cup shape. Take care not to distort the shape of the circle.

3 Use the large cutter to mark the side of the fish's head. Lightly press the small cutter into the top of the face for the eye, then mark a pupil with the tip of a large yarn needle. Repeat on the second piece, reversing the detail.

FISH

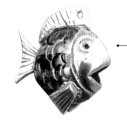

Tropical fish After polishing, color the fish in a variety of tropical colors using glass paints.

Applied eye You can alter the features by adding an applied ball of clay for the eye and varying the shape of the fins and tail.

Tools and materials

- Basic toolkit (see page 124)
- Silver clay: 5 g for rolling out (each fish uses 2 g or less)
- Round cutters: 1/2 in (13 mm) and 1/8 in (3 mm); you can use a fine drinking straw in place of the small cutter for marking eyes and scales
- Two spare round cutters or scraps of polymer clay to support marbles
- Two standard glass marbles: 5/8 in (15 mm)
- Templates: traced or photocopied and cut out
- Medium-grit sandpaper sheet

4 Use the edge of the small cutter or a drinking straw to mark scales on each circle, again reversing the detail for the second piece.

5 Cut out a notch from each piece for the mouth, matching the notches in size and position.

6 Roll out a sheet of clay, 4 p.c. (1 mm) thick. Using the templates, cut out the fins and tail. Use the large cutter to cut the lower curve of the top fin so that it matches the curve of the fish. Use a fine yarn needle to mark lines on both sides of the top fin and tail and to mark the hanging hole.

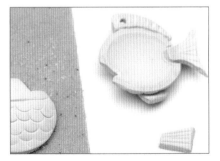

7 Dry all the pieces. Remove the fish sides from the marbles and rub them on sandpaper to smooth their edges. On one of the fish sides, file a notch on the back edge and paste the tail into it. Drill the hanging hole with a 1 mm bit and paste the top fin to the fish. Paste the side fins in place. Dry again.

8 Check that the two halves will fit together tightly, sanding further if needed, and then paste them together, matching the mouths. Fill any gaps with paste and dry. Sand away any excess and file the mouth opening if necessary to make it match. Fire and polish.

Bluebirds

Tiny bluebirds in flight are favorite charms and are symbols of happiness and good fortune. Blue resin is used to simulate enamel on the polished silver birds, and you can vary the design to make perching birds as well.

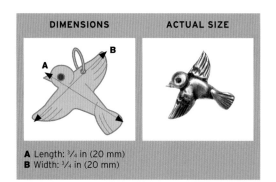

Tools and materials

- Basic toolkit (see page 124)
- Silver clay: about 3 g per bluebird
- Two-part clear coating resin
- Blue oil paint or resin pigment
- Mixing cup and spatula
- Rubbing alcohol and cotton swab
- Glass tumbler

DIMENSIONS	ACTUAL SIZE

A Length: ³⁄₄ in (20 mm)
B Width: ³⁄₄ in (20 mm)

1 Form an ¹⁄₈ in (3 mm) ball of clay and shape it into a teardrop. Pinch it between your finger and thumb to flatten it into a wing shape and press it down onto a ceramic tile, curved upward. Mark lines on it with a knife blade and feathers with the eye of a needle.

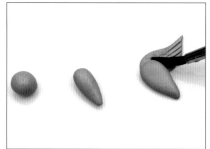

2 Form a ¹⁄₄ in (6 mm) ball of clay and shape it into a teardrop for the body. Brush water over the lower part of the wing and press the teardrop onto it with the point angled downward.

BLUEBIRDS

Perching bird *Make the bird more upright, omit the upper wing, and apply the lower wing to the body so that it angles backward. Insert a peg and loop finding for hanging.*

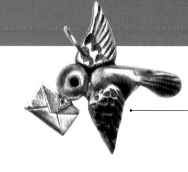

Bluebird with letter *Cut a small rectangle of clay and mark with lines to suggest an envelope. Paste under the beak before firing.*

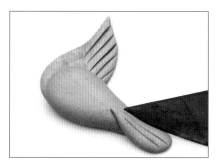

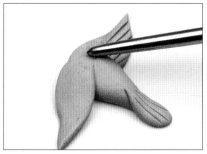

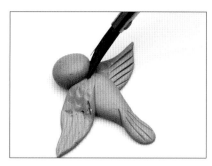

Antique bird *Oxidize the charm for an antique look.*

3 Form an ⅛ in (3 mm) ball of clay and shape it into a teardrop. Pinch it between a finger and thumb to flatten it for the tail. Brush the bottom of the body with water and press the tail, pointed end upward, onto the bottom of the body. Mark with lines to suggest feathers.

4 Brush water over the clay surface frequently as you work to keep the clay soft. Make another wing, the same as the first (see step 1), and press onto the wetted body, with the point angling forward and down. Mark lines and feathers as for the first wing.

5 Form a ³⁄₁₆ in (5 mm) ball of clay for the head, brush water on the top of the body, and press the head on.

Blue resin *Good quality oil paint can be used as a pigment, giving a huge palette of colors, such as this vivid blue.*

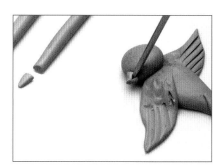

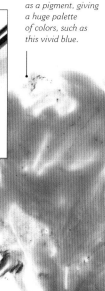

6 Roll a log of clay, ¹⁄₁₆ in (1.5 mm) thick, and point one end for the beak. Cut off the pointed end, about ¹⁄₁₆ in (1.5 mm) from the end. Push the cut side against the wetted head and use a darning needle to make a nostril, pushing the beak onto the head at the same time to secure.

7 Use a fine yarn needle to make a hole for the eye and mark a pilot hole in the front of the top wing for hanging. Dry the piece and then use a 1 mm bit to drill the hanging hole. Sand smooth and reinforce any cracks with paste.

8 Fire the bird and polish. Apply a thin coat of blue resin to color the bluebird (see page 31, steps 6–8).

Tools and materials

- Basic toolkit (see page 124)
- Silver clay: 5 g for rolling out (each horse uses 1 g or less)
- Templates: traced or photocopied and cut out
- Engraving tool such as a scribe or sharp-pointed burnisher

Horses

Sculpting a complete horse would be quite a challenge in miniature, but a horse's head is a simpler shape and can be cut out of a sheet of clay using a template. Add a bridle or a nameplate to personalize the charm for a horse-lover's particular equine friend.

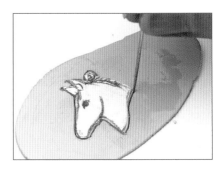

1 Roll out a sheet of clay, 2 p.c. (0.5 mm) thick. Smooth the clay onto a ceramic tile, oil the surface, and lay the horse head template on top. Use a fine sharp needle held vertically to cut around the template, wiping the needle frequently to remove any burrs of clays.

ACTUAL SIZE

TEMPLATES
Templates are shown actual size.

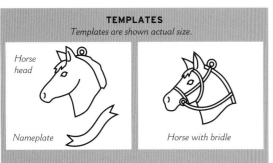

Horse head

Nameplate

Horse with bridle

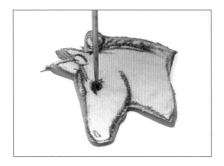

2 Peel away the waste clay, prick a hole through the horse's eye, and remove the template. Use a damp paintbrush to smooth over the cut edges. Trim away any excess clay with a knife.

3 Use a fine yarn needle to mark the lines of the horse's cheek and to define the ears, referring to the template as a guide. Use the needle to make a pilot hole in the hanging loop to be drilled later.

HORSES

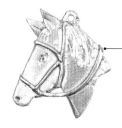

Bridle *Referring to the bridle template as a guide, cut thin strips from a 2 p.c. (0.5 mm) thick sheet of clay and use water to attach them to the head. For contrast, leave the horse with a satin finish and burnish the bridle only.*

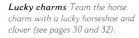

Lucky charms *Team the horse charm with a lucky horseshoe and clover (see pages 30 and 32).*

Mane *Personalize the charm by changing details such as the mane and forelock.*

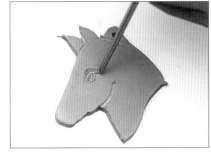

No nameplate *Omit the nameplate. If you wish, you can engrave the name of the horse on the back of the piece.*

4 Use the yarn needle to draw in the shape of the eye (the lines can be deepened after drying with an engraving tool). The blunt needle is less likely to make burrs of clay as you scribe, but if any appear, wipe them away with a damp paintbrush.

5 You can leave the horse's neck smooth, or draw lines to suggest a tumbling mane. Mark lines for the forelock on the horse's forehead.

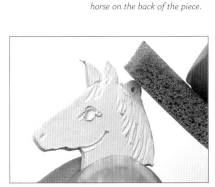

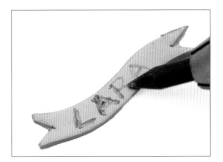

6 Dry the head on the tile and then deepen any engraved lines if necessary. Sand over the surface of the head and around the edges to smooth them. Use a needle file to file into any corners around the outline.

7 To make a nameplate, cut out the shape from a 2 p.c. (0.5 mm) thick sheet of clay using the template. Dry the plaque on the tile, write on the horse's name with a pencil, and then inscribe the letters with an engraving tool.

8 Paste the nameplate to the bottom of the horse's neck and dry again. Check that the back is neat, reinforce the join with paste if required, and then dry. Fire and polish, then oxidize to bring out the detail.

Owls

Owls are much-loved birds and popular ornaments. These owl charms are sculpted directly in silver clay, so make sure that the clay is well hydrated before you begin or it will become too dry as you work. If you prefer, you can sculpt the owl in polymer clay, which is easier to work with, and then make a mold using polymer clay (see page 34) or putty silicone (see page 40). However, the owl will need to be flatter in order to make a successful mold.

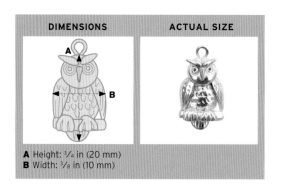

DIMENSIONS   **ACTUAL SIZE**

A Height: ³/₄ in (20 mm)
B Width: ³/₈ in (10 mm)

Tools and materials

- Basic toolkit (see page 124)
- Silver clay: 3 g per owl
- Brush protector, metal tube, or ballpoint pen refill, ³/₃₂ in (2 mm) wide, for marking eyes
- Peg and loop finding

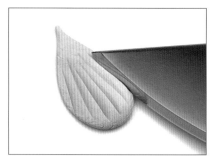

1 Form an ¹/₈ in (3 mm) ball of clay and point one end to make a teardrop. Press it onto a ceramic tile, point upward, for the owl's tail. Mark vertical lines on the tail with a craft knife.

2 Form a ¹/₄ in (6 mm) ball of clay and shape into an oval for the body. Brush water on the top of the tail and press on the body. Use the eye of a darning needle to mark feathers on the body.

OWLS

Jeweled eyes *Press 2 mm fireable gemstones or glass beads into the owl's eyes before drying and firing. Oxidize the owl to color it and then varnish.*

Golden owl *Paint varnish onto the eye circles, allow to dry, and then oxidize the owl until it is a golden color. Varnish over the color to preserve it.*

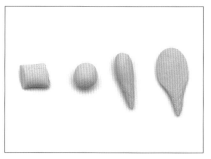

3 Roll a log of clay, ⅛ in (3 mm) thick, and cut two ⅛ in (3 mm) lengths. Roll each of these into a ball, then point one end to make a teardrop and squeeze between thumb and forefinger to flatten into a wing shape.

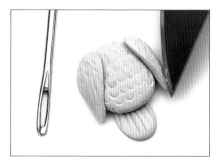

4 Brush water on either side of the body and press on the wings, points downward. Use the needle eye to mark feathers on the top of the wings; use the knife to mark lines on the bottom to suggest long wing feathers.

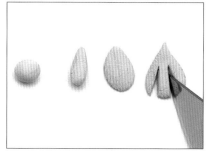

5 Roll a log of clay, ¹⁄₁₆ in (1.5 mm) thick, and cut two ⅛ in (3 mm) lengths for the feet. Shape into teardrops and press down onto the tile, points upward. Cut two vertical lines in the bottom of each and ease the clay apart to make claws.

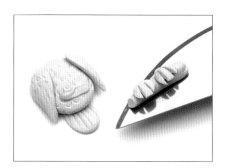

6 To make a branch, cut a ⅜ in (10 mm) length from the ¹⁄₁₆ in (1.5 mm) thick log and brush with water. Slide the knife blade under each foot and curve the feet around the branch. Brush paste on the bottom of the owl's body and press the branch onto it.

7 Brush water on the neck and press on a ¼ in (6 mm) ball of clay for the head. Use a tube to mark eyes and a fine yarn needle to add pupils. Form a tiny teardrop, cut off the point for the beak, and attach it to the face with water; use a paintbrush and knife tip to ease it into place.

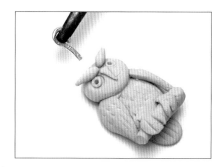

8 Cut two ¹⁄₁₆ in (1.5 mm) lengths from a log of the same thickness and shape each into a teardrop. Use water to attach them above the eyes, points angled out and upward. Push a peg and loop finding into the top of the head. Dry, fire, and polish.

Steampunk turtles

Tools and materials

- Basic toolkit (see page 124)
- Silver clay: 2.5 g per turtle
- Watch parts: available from jewelry-making suppliers or break up an old clockwork watch
- Polymer clay for making texture sheet
- Talcum powder
- Peg and loop finding

Clockwork watch parts are a popular feature of steampunk design, and here they are used to texture the shell of a turtle charm. Steampunk is a fascinating mixture of antique and science fiction, incorporating motifs from 19th-century industrial machinery into whimsical designs. When making the texture sheet, use a fine needle point to help you lift the watch parts out of the polymer clay before baking.

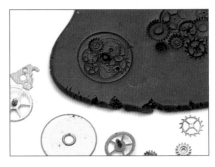

1 Roll out the polymer clay, 8 p.c. (2 mm) thick, and smooth it down onto a ceramic tile. Dust with talcum powder and push watch parts into the surface to make an interesting texture. Remove the watch parts and bake the clay as recommended on the package.

Copper turtle *Oxidize to a metallic copper color to complement the industrial steampunk theme.*

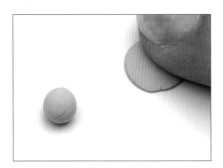

2 Form a ³/₁₆ in (5 mm) ball of silver clay and press it down on a tile to make a ³/₈ in (10 mm) disk for the base of the turtle.

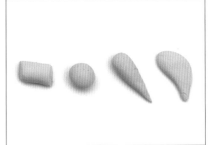

3 Roll a log of silver clay, ¹/₈ in (3 mm) thick, and cut two ³/₁₆ in (5 mm) lengths for the front flippers. Shape each into a ball, then a teardrop, and press onto the tile, curving the point down.

STEAMPUNK TURTLES

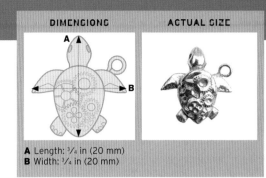

DIMENSIONS   ACTUAL SIZE

A Length: ¾ in (20 mm)
B Width: ¾ in (20 mm)

Sea turtle Oxidize to a blue green color and then polish back to accentuate the details of the design.

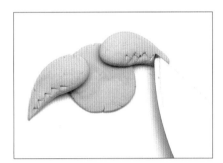

4 Brush water over the disk and press the teardrops onto it, pointing outward. Flatten each into a flipper shape and mark details with the tip of a craft knife.

5 Cut two ⅛ in (3 mm) lengths from the same log and pinch one end into a rounded point. Press these onto the bottom of the wetted disk, flat ends downward and splayed, for the back legs. Reinforce the joins with paste. Mark the toes with the knife.

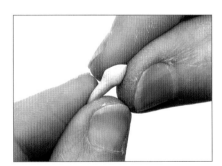

6 Form a ¼ in (6 mm) ball of clay. Roll one end thinner for the neck and pinch the other end into a turtle head shape. Press the neck onto the wetted disk between the front flippers so that the head protrudes. Pierce an eye on either side with a fine yarn needle.

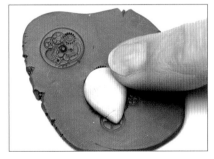

7 Form a ¼ in (6 mm) ball of clay and shape into a teardrop. Oil the surface and push it down firmly onto the texture sheet so that it forms a textured flattened shape large enough to cover the tops of the flippers and legs for the shell.

8 Brush paste over the neck and tops of the limbs, then push the shell down to secure everything with the textured side uppermost. Push a peg and loop finding into one flipper and dry. Reinforce the joins underneath with paste if needed, then fire and polish.

Heart frame Use two sizes of heart cutter to cut out the front of the frame. Before removing the waste clay from around the outside, cut out a hanging loop to fit in the top of the heart. This is easier than cutting it to fit.

Tools and materials

- Basic toolkit (see page 124)
- Silver clay: 5 g for rolling out (each frame uses 1.5 g, but quantity will vary according to size of frame being made)
- Square cutter: 3/8 in (10 mm)
- Round cutter: 3/16 in (5 mm)
- Photograph with the image of the head about 1/4 in (6 mm) high, or to fit in the area of the cutter
- White polymer clay: 1/8 of a 2 oz (56 g) block
- Craft glue
- Epoxy glue or superglue
- Acrylic varnish

Picture frames

Make a family heirloom charm with these tiny frames. Polymer clay is used as the backing to save on silver clay. While these charms are fairly robust, do not immerse in water during wear or the photos may deteriorate. For a more permanent charm, use transfer paper such as Lazertran to transfer the image onto soft polymer clay before making the backing. After baking, the image will be permanently embedded in the polymer clay backing.

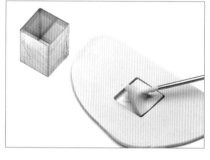

1 Roll out a sheet of silver clay, 4 p.c. (1 mm) thick. Smooth it onto a ceramic tile and cut out a square in the center with a cutter. Allow to air dry for a few minutes, then pierce the square with a darning needle held at a shallow angle and lift it clear.

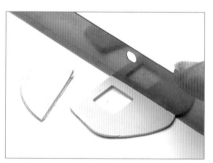

2 Use a straight blade to cut around the cutout square to leave an 1/8 in (3 mm) wide frame on all sides. Do not move the frame or it will distort.

PICTURE FRAMES

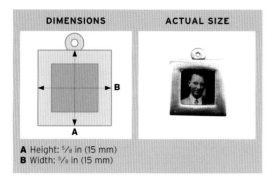

DIMENSIONS | **ACTUAL SIZE**

A Height: ⁵⁄₈ in (15 mm)
B Width: ⁵⁄₈ in (15 mm)

Floral frame Texture the sheet of silver clay with a floral texture sheet.

Round frame
Texture the sheet of silver clay and use two round cutters, one larger than the other, to cut out the front of the frame.

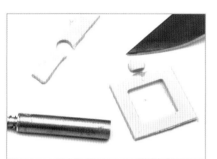

3 Place the round cutter just over the edge of the leftover clay sheet, cut out a clay tag, and paste the straight edge of the tag to the frame (see page 130). Use a fine yarn needle to make a pilot hole.

4 Dry the frame on the tile, then sand to smooth the edges. Drill the hole in the clay tag with a 1 mm bit and use a needle file to smooth the cut edge inside the frame. Fire the frame and then brush and polish it to the desired finish.

5 Lay the frame on the photograph, positioning the face inside the square, and draw around the outside edge with a fine pencil. Cut out the photograph inside the pencil line and then check that it fits well inside the frame area.

6 Roll out the polymer clay, 2 p.c. (0.5 mm) thick. Smooth the clay onto a tile, press the empty silver frame on top, and trim the clay neatly and precisely around the frame. Make a hole through the polymer clay behind the clay tag.

7 Bake the polymer clay with the frame in place as recommended on the package. When cool, slide a blade underneath to free it from the tile. Glue the photograph to the back of the silver frame with craft glue and allow to dry.

8 Glue the frame to the polymer clay backing with epoxy or superglue, taking care not to fill the hanging hole. Coat the front of the photograph with varnish for permanence (or use clear coating resin if you prefer).

100

Silhouettes

Tools and materials

- Basic toolkit (see page 124)
- Silver clay: 5 g for rolling out (each silhouette uses about 1.5 g, but quantity will vary according to size of charm being made)
- Photograph of the subject in profile, reduced on a photocopier or computer to about ¾ in (20 mm) high and printed on ordinary copier paper
- Engraving tool such as a scribe or sharp-pointed burnisher
- Peg and loop finding

Silhouette portraits have a long history and first became popular in the 18th century as framed pictures. Silhouette heads of children cut out of silver and gold to make charms became popular in the 20th century, and here is the modern version using silver clay. You will need a steady hand, but it is far easier to cut the shape out of clay than to saw it out of sheet metal.

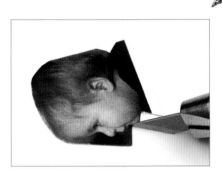

1 Cut out the photograph around the outline of the head and face using a fine knife blade or scalpel. Take care over the tiny details because this will make a better likeness.

2 Roll out a sheet of clay, 2 p.c. (0.5 mm) thick. Smooth it onto a ceramic tile, oil the surface, and lay the portrait on top. Use a fine sharp needle held vertically to cut around it. Wipe the needle frequently to remove burrs of clay.

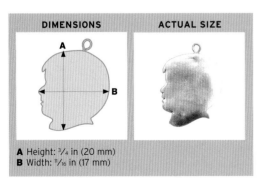

DIMENSIONS	ACTUAL SIZE

A Height: ¾ in (20 mm)
B Width: ¹¹⁄₁₆ in (17 mm)

Engraving Engrave the back of the silhouette with the name of the child. You could also add the child's age or the date of the photograph.

SILHOUETTES

Long hair
*Simplify hair
into single locks
that can be cut
out of the clay.*

Map *Use a reduced map of a
state or country (this one is Italy)
as a template to make a map
silhouette charm. Engrave the
charm with the dates of a special
vacation or event.*

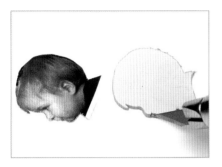

3 Remove the photograph and waste clay, then work around the edges of the clay with the knife to correct the shape. Keep laying the photograph back on the clay to check the profile. Cut the bottom edge into an attractive curve.

4 Brush over the cut edges with a damp paintbrush to smooth away any rough areas. Be careful around the face so that you do not alter the profile.

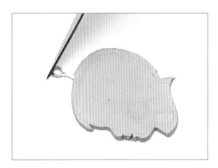

5 Push a peg and loop finding into the top of the head and smooth the surface if it bulges. If the peg is not fully embedded on the back, you can paste over it after drying.

6 Dry the piece on the tile, then lightly sand over the surface to smooth it. Sand any rough edges, but take care not to alter the outline. Paste over the peg finding on the back if it did not embed fully in the clay when you pushed it in.

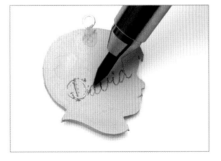

7 Write the child's name on the back in pencil, then inscribe with an engraving tool. Work over each letter several times, brushing the dust away with a paintbrush. Correct errors with paste and sand smooth again.

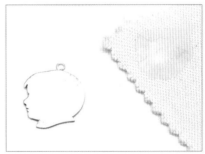

8 Fire the piece and polish either to a mirror finish or leave as a satin finish. Burnish all around the edge of the piece to make it shine.

Tools and materials

- Basic toolkit (see page 124)
- Silver clay: 5 g for rolling out (each letter charm uses 1.5 g)
- Peg-type rubber stamps: ½ in (13 mm)
- Round cutter: ½ in (13 mm)
- Sheet of small letters in attractive fonts, about ¼ in (6 mm) high, printed from a computer or photocopied from a book
- Acrylic varnish
- Two-part clear coating resin
- Mixing cup and spatula
- Glass tumbler

Letters

Creating an alphabet of charms opens a world of possibilities. You can make initial letter charms, write messages in charms, spell out names, and more. This project uses paper cutouts of printed letters set in resin on a silver tag charm. The resin is domed over the letter to give a jewel-like magnifying effect, and the back of the charm is impressed with a stamp as decoration.

Texture *Decorate the back of the charm using a texture sheet.*

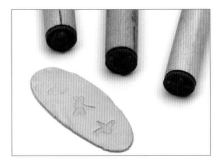

1 Roll out a sheet of clay, 4 p.c. (1 mm) thick. Smooth the clay onto a ceramic tile and lightly oil the surface. Stamp images into the clay to decorate the backs of the charms. Do not press too hard or the stamp will go right through the clay and make a hole.

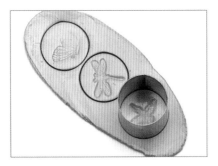

2 Cut out circles using a round cutter, positioning the cutter carefully over each stamped image. Remove the waste clay and then dry the pieces. When they can be moved without distorting them, turn them over so that the stamped side is face down.

3 Roll out a sheet of clay, 6 p.c. (1.5 mm) thick, and cut an ⅛ in (3 mm) wide strip. Cut off ⅛ in (3 mm) squares for hanging loops. Wet the side of each stamped circle and press on a square. Trim the corners to round them and use a fine yarn needle make a pilot hole in the center.

4 Dry all the pieces again and then sand off any rough edges. Drill the hole with a 1 mm bit, then fire and polish. Making the hanging loops from a thicker sheet of clay creates a lip that will prevent the resin from flowing into the hole.

LETTERS

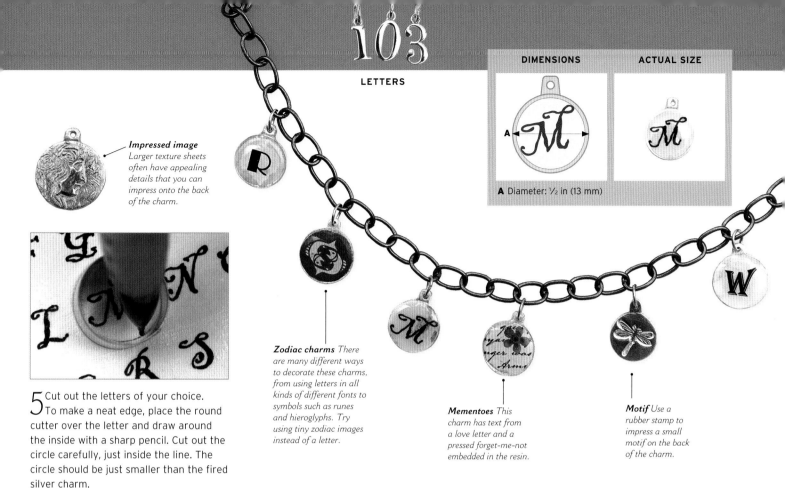

Impressed image Larger texture sheets often have appealing details that you can impress onto the back of the charm.

DIMENSIONS	ACTUAL SIZE

A Diameter: ½ in (13 mm)

Zodiac charms There are many different ways to decorate these charms, from using letters in all kinds of different fonts to symbols such as runes and hieroglyphs. Try using tiny zodiac images instead of a letter.

Mementoes This charm has text from a love letter and a pressed forget-me-not embedded in the resin.

Motif Use a rubber stamp to impress a small motif on the back of the charm.

5 Cut out the letters of your choice. To make a neat edge, place the round cutter over the letter and draw around the inside with a sharp pencil. Cut out the circle carefully, just inside the line. The circle should be just smaller than the fired silver charm.

6 The paper must be sealed on all sides, so paint the back with varnish and press down onto the charm. Varnish the top and edges and allow to dry. Mix some resin according to the instructions on the package and allow to rest for about 10 minutes for the bubbles to disperse.

7 Apply resin with a large yarn needle, spreading it over the paper and doming it about ⅛ in (3 mm) high. Do not apply too thickly or it will flow off. The slight lip should prevent it from flooding into the hanging hole, but if it does, wipe it off and reapply with less resin.

8 Cover the pieces with an upside down glass tumbler to keep dust off and allow the resin to set (usually about 24 hours). If you want a higher dome to your pieces, apply a second layer of resin when the first layer is completely set.

Fingerprints

Silver clay has always been popular as a material for taking imprints of fingerprints for jewelry. It is expensive to have this done commercially, but you can do it yourself for a fraction of the price. The fine-textured clay takes a good impression and, after firing and polishing, it makes a perfect keepsake charm of babies, children, and loved ones.

Tools and materials

- Basic toolkit (see page 124)
- Silver clay: at least 7 g for rolling out thickly enough to take a fingerprint and cut out a shape (each charm uses about 5 g, depending on size of fingerprint and cutter used)
- Cutter to suit size of fingerprint: a ¾ in (20 mm) cutter is suitable for babies and children under about 5 years; older children will need a 1 in (25 mm) cutter
- Engraving tool such as a scribe or sharp-pointed burnisher

1 Roll out the clay, 6 p.c. (1.5 mm) thick. Smooth the clay onto a ceramic tile and lightly smear the surface with oil.

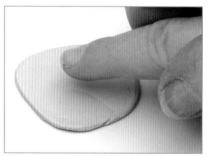

2 For a young child: With the child on your lap, tuck back all the fingers except the index finger. Hold the other hand back to prevent unwanted help and press the index finger into the clay, pressing it down if necessary. Remove by lifting up vertically to prevent smudging.

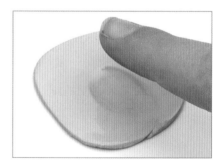

3 For an older child: Ask the child to press an index finger into the clay and rock it slightly to get a good impression. Remove the finger and check the imprint. If it is not clear, re-roll the clay and try again. Children usually enjoy the process and are happy to have another try.

DIMENSIONS | ACTUAL SIZE

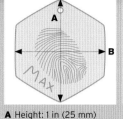

A Height: 1 in (25 mm)
B Width: 1 in (25 mm)

FINGERPRINTS

Shape variations
Vary the cutter used to cut out the charm, such as a star or flower shape.

Gemstones *Press a fireable gemstone into the charm before drying and firing. The child's birthstone would be particularly appropriate.*

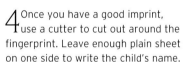

4 Once you have a good imprint, use a cutter to cut out around the fingerprint. Leave enough plain sheet on one side to write the child's name.

5 Carefully peel away the waste clay from around the cutout shape. The piece must remain on the tile until it is dry.

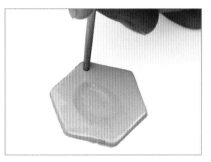

6 Use a fine yarn needle to make a pilot hole at an appropriate point for hanging the charm. Dry the piece on the tile.

7 Sand around the edges of the charm to smooth them, but take care not to sand over the area of the fingerprint. Drill the hanging hole with a 1 mm drill bit.

8 Write the child's name in pencil around the edge of the charm, then inscribe the letters with an engraving tool. Add a date and other motifs if you wish. Fire and then polish around the fingerprint, avoiding the print itself. Oxidize and polish back to accentuate the fingerprint.

MONTH	ARTIFICIAL GEMSTONE
January	Garnet (dark red)
February	Amethyst (purple)
March	Aquamarine (aqua blue)
April	Diamond (white)
May	Emerald (green; see note below)
June	Alexandrite (pale mauve)
July	Ruby (red)
August	Peridot (pale yellow-green)
September	Sapphire (deep blue)
October	Pink tourmaline (pink)
November	Topaz (pale yellow-orange)
December	Zircon (pale blue)

NOTE *Check that stones are fireable with your supplier. Do not fire natural precious stones because they may disintegrate in the heat. Green stones such as emerald are not normally fireable, so glue in after firing.*

KEEPSAKE CHARMS

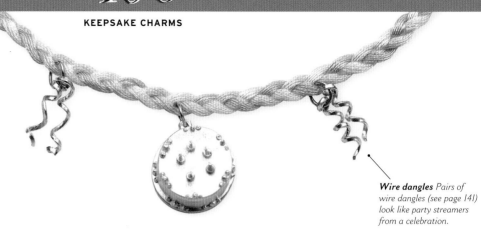

Wire dangles *Pairs of wire dangles (see page 141) look like party streamers from a celebration.*

Tools and materials

- Basic toolkit (see page 124)
- Silver clay: 7 g for rolling out (each cake uses 4.5 g)
- Round cutters: 3/4 in (20 mm) and 1/2 in (13 mm)
- Silver clay syringe with fine (0.5 mm) nozzle

Birthday cakes

Cake charms make perfect birthday gifts and the basic cake can be decorated in different ways to suit other occasions. Five candles are shown in the project steps here, but you can use more or fewer if you wish. The cake is hollow to make it lighter and save on clay.

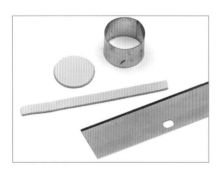

1 Roll out a sheet of clay, 4 p.c. (1 mm) thick. Smooth the clay onto a ceramic tile and cut out a circle for the cake board using the largest cutter. Carefully remove the waste clay. Using a straight blade, cut a 3/16 x 2 in (5 x 50 mm) strip from the same sheet for the cake sides.

2 Wet one side of the strip and wrap it around the medium cutter, aligning one long edge against the edge of the cutter. Overlap the ends, cut through both layers, and remove the excess, leaving the rest of the strip on the cutter to dry.

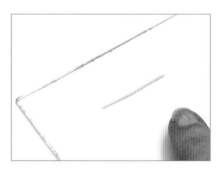

3 Roll a log of clay for the candles, 1/32 in (1 mm) thick. Use a log roller to smooth it and make it a little thinner. You will need about a 1 in (25 mm) length. Place the log on the tile and push the edge of a rolling guide against it to make it straight.

DIMENSIONS	ACTUAL SIZE
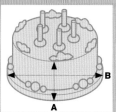	

A Height: 5/16 in (8 mm)
B Diameter: 3/4 in (20 mm)

Decorations *Try decorating the cake in different ways. Here, a continuous line of dots has been piped around the base and top edge.*

4 Dry all the pieces. Remove the strip from the cutter (this should be easy because it is not joined). Use paste to join the two ends and hold the gap closed until it sets (you can place the ring between two tiles pushed together).

5 To make the cake top, roll out a sheet of clay, 4 p.c. (1 mm) thick. Lay it on a tile and wet the surface. Press the cake sides onto the sheet and reinforce inside with paste to make a good join. Trim all around the cake sides and then dry the piece on the tile.

Wedding cake *Make extra tiers for the cake, either in the same way or by cutting smaller circles out of a 12 p.c. (3 mm) thick sheet of clay. Decorate the cake with a bow (see page 61).*

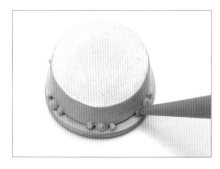

6 Sand all the pieces to smooth rough areas. Brush paste around the bottom of the cake sides and press onto the center of the cake board. Syringe dots of clay in groups of three around the base and top edge of the cake for the iced decoration.

7 Cut the dried candle log into five 1/8 in (3 mm) lengths. The log should cut neatly, but you can sand the ends lightly to make them flat. Make a clay tag and attach it to the side of the cake board (see page 130); use a fine yarn needle to mark it with a pilot hole.

8 Syringe a circle of five large dots on top of the cake, insert a candle into each one, and hold upright until it sets. Dry again, then drill the clay tag with a 1 mm bit. Fire, brush, and polish. You can leave the top surface of the cake unbrushed so that it remains frosty white.

Champagne glasses

These tiny champagne glass charms would be suitable as a wedding gift or for any special occasion. They are based on a vintage glass design with an open bowl, which is easier to make in silver clay than a modern flute. The bowls of the glasses are made using a round glass bead as a form. Try to find a bead that is as spherical as possible.

Tools and materials

- Basic toolkit (see page 124)
- Silver clay: 5 g for rolling out (each glass uses 1.5 g)
- Round glass bead: ³⁄₈ in (10 mm)
- Round cutters: ¹⁄₂ in (13 mm) and ¹⁄₄ in (6 mm)
- Scrap of polymer clay
- Ball-headed tool: ¹⁄₈ in (3 mm)
- Fine-grit sandpaper sheet
- Silver clay syringe with medium (1 mm) nozzle

DIMENSIONS

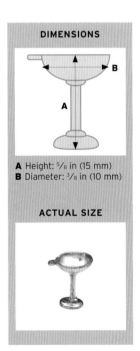

A Height: ⁵⁄₈ in (15 mm)
B Diameter: ³⁄₈ in (10 mm)

ACTUAL SIZE

1 Press some polymer clay into the bead's hole to fill it so that the silver clay will not get into the hole. Smooth away any excess. (Most beads with holes have slightly flattened ends on which you can stand them; if your bead does not, prop it in a round cutter.)

Champagne bubbles
Partly fill the bowl with tiny clear glass seed beads to suggest champagne bubbles. Fill the glass with resin lightly colored yellow, or add a touch of pink for pink champagne.

2 Roll out a sheet of silver clay, 2 p.c. (0.5 mm) thick, and cut out a circle with the large cutter. Smooth the clay circle onto the bead to form a cup shape and indent the center with a ball tool.

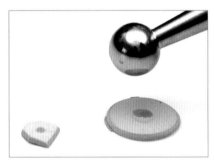

3 Using the same sheet, cut out a circle with the small cutter for the foot of the glass. Press it down with your finger to chamfer the edges, then indent the center with the ball tool. Cut an ¹⁄₈ in (3 mm) clay tag for hanging and mark it with a pilot hole (see page 130).

Heart glass *Attach a tiny red polymer clay heart with jump rings to the glass stem.*

4 Roll a log for the glass stem, $1/32$ in (1 mm) thick and about 1 in (25 mm) long. Use a log roller to make it even. Place the log on a ceramic tile and push the edge of a rolling guide against it to make it straight. Dry all the pieces.

5 Remove the clay bowl from the bead, using a craft knife to cut away the polymer clay if it is attached. Rub the edge of the bowl in a circular motion on a sheet of sandpaper to straighten the rim. Sand all the pieces to smooth any rough edges.

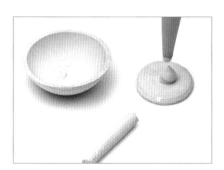

6 Cut a $3/8$ in (10 mm) length from the glass stem log and sand the ends to make sure that they are at right angles to the stem. Syringe a blob of clay onto the top of the glass foot and press on the stem, holding it upright until it sets, then dry fully.

7 Syringe a blob of clay onto the base of the glass bowl and press onto the stem, again holding until it sets. You will need to view the glass from all sides to make sure that the stem is vertical. After firing, you can bend it slightly to adjust if necessary.

8 Drill the hole in the clay tag with a 1 mm bit and paste it just below the rim of the glass bowl. Dry fully with a heat gun or in the oven, and then fire with the glass on its bowl to avoid sagging. Polish to a high shine.

Gemstone beads

Bead charms are relatively new types of charms that have rapidly become established as favorites. The beads come in a wonderful variety of designs and all have a large hole through which a chain or cord is threaded to wear as a bracelet or necklace. Making your own silver clay bead charms is not difficult and you can personalize them in many ways. See page 105 for the birthstones to use for birthday bead charms.

DIMENSIONS	ACTUAL SIZE
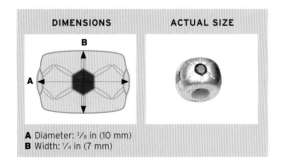	

A Diameter: ³/₈ in (10 mm)
B Width: ¹/₄ in (7 mm)

1 Hydrate the clay well and form it into a ³/₈ in (10 mm) ball. Smear the top with oil and place it on your work surface. Push the cutter straight down into the center of the ball.

2 Twisting it carefully, push the ball of clay farther onto the cutter; the oil will help it slide on. Use the plunger to push out the plug of clay from the cutter (or a yarn needle if you are using a tube).

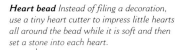

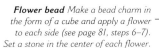

Star points *File more star points around the gemstone holes to increase the sparkle effect.*

Heart bead *Instead of filing a decoration, use a tiny heart cutter to impress little hearts all around the bead while it is soft and then set a stone into each heart.*

Flower bead *Make a bead charm in the form of a cube and apply a flower to each side (see page 81, steps 6–7). Set a stone in the center of each flower.*

Stone size and color *Try changing the color of the stones, or using a variety of stones in different sizes.*

3 Mark four holes evenly spaced around the bead with a large yarn needle. This will make drilling holes for the stones easier when the clay is dry. Allow the piece to dry for a while to firm up, then gently twist it off the cutter and dry fully.

4 Sand over the piece to remove any blemishes. Drill holes with a 2 mm bit right through the pilot needle holes to the large inner hole of the bead. This will let light into the back of the stones after setting and give more sparkle.

5 Use a stone setting burr to drill into the top of each drill hole. Each hole should be deep enough for the stone to sit in with its flat top (table) just below the surface of the surrounding clay.

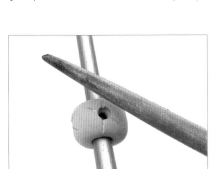

6 Use the edge of a needle file to file star points around each hole, lining up the file carefully across the hole. This adds a lively sparkle to the mounted gemstone.

7 Push a stone into each hole. This is easiest if you place the stone on your work surface with the pointed bottom (pavilion) upward and press the hole over it. When the clay shrinks during firing, the stone will be gripped tight in the hole.

8 Fire the piece but do not quench because this may crack the stones. Polish the finished bead.

Tools and materials

- Basic toolkit (see page 124)
- Silver clay: 5 g for making charm (each fruit bead uses 4 g; 1 g is cut out for central hole)
- Round tube cutter with plunger or 1 in (25 mm) long metal tube: ³/₁₆ in (5 mm)
- Ball-headed tool: ¹/₈ in (3 mm)
- Glass paints: red and green for a strawberry
- Rubbing alcohol and cotton swab
- Varnish suitable for metal

Fruit

Bead charms lend themselves to organic shapes, and the luscious colors of fruits make these charms ideal for jewelry. The strawberry charm demonstrated can easily be adapted to create other fruits. Using a tube to make the large bead hole is easiest with firm clay. If you find it difficult to push the tube through or are using a softer clay, try the paintbrush handle technique (see page 114, step 1).

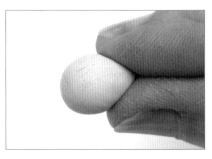

1 Form a ³/₈ in (10 mm) ball of clay and pinch the bottom into a rounded point to make a strawberry shape.

2 Lightly oil the cutter and clay surface. Push the cutter into the side of the upper part of the strawberry, twisting as you push. When you reach the center, twist the cutter out again.

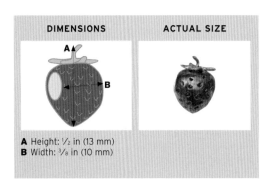

DIMENSIONS	ACTUAL SIZE

A Height: ½ in (13 mm)
B Width: ³/₈ in (10 mm)

FRUIT

Grapes *Make a basic bead in the same way as the strawberry, but smaller and slimmer with more of a point downward. Roll ⅟₁₆ in (1.5 mm) balls of clay and attach with paste all over the bead. Cut a vine leaf shape from a 2 p.c. (0.5 mm) thick sheet of clay, mark with veins, and paste to the top. Fire and polish, then paint with purple and green glass paints.*

Lemon *Pinch the basic bead into a pointed shape at both top and bottom to make a lemon shape. Press a wire brush all over the clay surface to texture it. Cut a simple leaf shape, mark with veins, and paste to the top of the bead. Fire and polish, then paint with yellow and green glass paints.*

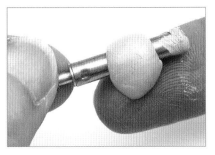

3 Use the plunger to push out the plug of clay from the cutter (or a yarn needle if you are using a tube). Clean the cutter well and push it into the other side of the bead, opposite the first hole, and keep twisting until the cutter emerges on the other side.

4 Remove the cutter and clean it, then push it back into the bead to provide support. Impress seed marks all over the strawberry with the eye of a darning needle, making them smaller and closer together at the bottom.

5 Indent the center top of the berry with a ball tool. Smooth the bead with a wet finger slicked over the surface if it shows any cracks or dry areas.

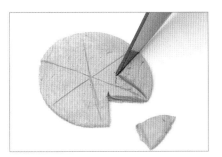

6 Form a ¼ in (6 mm) ball of clay and press it down onto a ceramic tile to form a ⅜ in (10 mm) disk. Mark across the center three times. Cut out wedges between pairs of lines to make a star-shaped calyx (or use a star cutter).

7 Apply paste in the center top of the strawberry and press the calyx into this. Use a yarn needle to accentuate the veins. Roll a log of clay, ⅟₃₂ in (1 mm) thick, and cut an ⅛ in (3 mm) length for a stalk. Paste this to the center of the calyx.

8 Dry thoroughly and sand any rough areas, then fire and polish. Use a cotton swab to degrease the surface with alcohol. Paint with red and green glass paints, bake if recommended on the package, and then varnish.

Skulls

The skull is an age-old symbol that is found in many decorative forms. It is carved on gravestones to symbolize mortality and the afterlife; worn for magical protection as a talisman; used as an emblem of bravado and defiance on pirate flags; and, in recent times, has been a ubiquitous image in gothic fashion. The shape of the skull lends itself well to bead charms, and this project shows you how to sculpt a simple skull from clay.

Tools and materials

- Basic toolkit (see page 124)
- Silver clay: 7 g for making charm (each skull uses 6 g; 1 g is cut out for central hole)
- Paintbrush handle, about ³⁄₁₆ in (5 mm) thick
- Ball-headed tool: ¹⁄₈ in (3 mm)

Skull and crossbones
Sculpt simple long bones in silver clay and attach to the bottom of the skull with paste before firing.

1 Roll a ¹⁄₂ in (13 mm) ball of clay and point one end slightly to form an egg shape. Oil the clay surface and push a large yarn needle through the wider part of the egg shape. Enlarge the hole a little with the needle, then replace it with the oiled paintbrush handle.

2 Make sure that the hole is in the upper half of the shape so that the skull will hang the right way up. Pinch the clay back to an egg shape on the handle if it has distorted, and use a ball tool to make two eye sockets just above the middle line on the front of the egg.

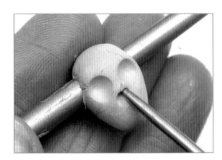

3 Make the nose cavity by pushing the needle twice into the center of the face, just below the eye sockets. Lift the clay above the nose with the needle to suggest a nasal bone.

SKULLS

DIMENSIONS	ACTUAL SIZE

A Height: ¾ in (20 mm)
B Width: ½ in (13 mm)

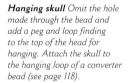

Hanging skull *Omit the hole made through the bead and add a peg and loop finding to the top of the head for hanging. Attach the skull to the hanging loop of a converter bead (see page 118).*

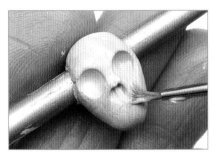

4 Brush the surface of the skull with a damp paintbrush to keep the clay moist and to smooth away any cracks.

5 Hollow out the cheeks on either side of the face and under the eye sockets with the ball tool. Indent slightly above the eye sockets as well.

6 Pinch the chin to make it protrude farther and then cut a horizontal slash across the face below the nose for the mouth. Twist the knife blade to open the mouth a little.

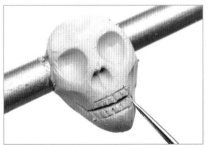

7 Use a darning needle to mark a horizontal line above and below the mouth, and then mark vertical lines for the teeth.

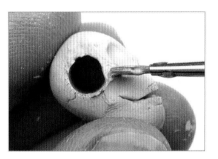

8 Remove the handle from the bead hole and brush over the area around the hole on both sides to smooth. Dry thoroughly, fire, and polish. Oxidize to emphasize the eye sockets and cavities.

Tools and materials

- Basic toolkit
  (see page 124)
- Silver clay:
  10 g for making
  the initial block
  (each house uses
  4–6 g, depending
  on decorations)
- Round tube cutter
  with plunger or 1 in
  (25 mm) long metal
  tube: $^3/_{16}$ in (5 mm)

Little houses

Miniature houses make enchanting bead charms and can be decorated in a variety of ways. They are made by stacking sheets of clay together to create a firm block with squarer edges than could be achieved by simply shaping a block of clay. Use slightly firm clay that is not too moist, and make sure that the hole is in the top half of the house or it will not hang the right way.

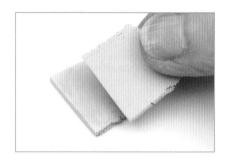

1 Roll out a sheet of clay, 8 p.c. (2 mm) thick. Cut it in half and smear the surface of one half with water. Press on the other half and trim to $^5/_{16}$ x $^5/_8$ in (8 x 15 mm).

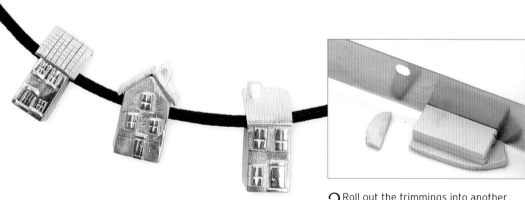

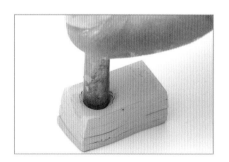

2 Roll out the trimmings into another sheet of the same thickness and smear with water. Lay on the block of clay and cut around to add another layer. Repeat to add a fourth layer. The block should be about $^5/_{16}$ x $^5/_{16}$ x $^5/_8$ in (8 x 8 x 15 mm).

3 Trim the sides further if required— there may be lines showing from the layers. Push the cutter or tube into the top half of the block to make the bead hole. Twist the cutter to remove it and push out the clay in the cutter for use in other projects.

LITTLE HOUSES

Engraved details *After drying, use an engraving tool such as a scribe or sharp-pointed burnisher to inscribe the outlines and details of the windows and door. Paste a thin strip of clay sheet under each window for a window ledge.*

Pitched roof *Cut the roof angle into a point and apply two sheets of clay for the roof. Try altering the details to make different arrangements of windows and door.*

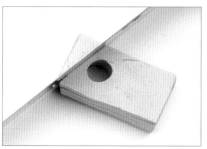

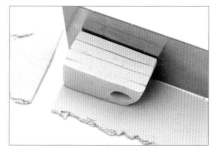

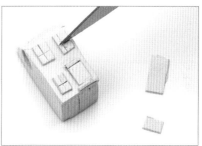

4 To make a sloping roof, use a straight blade to cut the top of the block at an angle, 1/32 in (1 mm) away from the hole. The front of the house will be the short side resulting from this cut. Lightly dry the piece to firm it up.

5 Roll out a sheet of clay, 2 p.c. (0.5 mm) thick. Brush water over the front of the block, press it onto the sheet, and trim around it to give the house a smooth front. Dry fully and then sand any rough areas. Use paste to fill any gaps, then dry and sand again.

6 Roll out a sheet of clay, 2 p.c. (0.5 mm) thick. Cut 1/8 x 5/32 in (3 x 4 mm) rectangles for the windows and a longer rectangle for the door. Attach to the house front with water. Cut small strips to apply above and below the door and mark windowpanes with a cross. Use a darning needle to mark a doorknob.

7 Cut a roof from the same sheet, slightly larger than the sloping top of the house. Mark it with lines or squares to suggest roof tiles. Dry lightly and then paste to the top of the house so that it overlaps at the front and sides.

8 Roll out some clay, 8 p.c. (2 mm) thick, and cut a tiny rectangular block from it, about 1/8 in (3 mm) high and 3/32 in (2 mm) wide. Cut the bottom edge at the same angle as the roof and paste in place for the chimney. Fill any gaps around the roof with paste, then dry and fire.

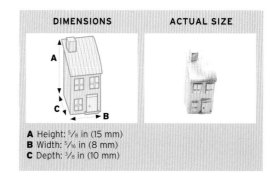

DIMENSIONS	ACTUAL SIZE

A Height: 5/8 in (15 mm)
B Width: 5/16 in (8 mm)
C Depth: 3/8 in (10 mm)

Converter beads

Tools and materials

- Basic toolkit (see page 124)
- Silver clay: 5 g for rolling out (each large bail uses 2 g; each small bead uses 1 g)
- Texture sheet or rubber stamp with ⁵⁄₈ in (15 mm) circle motif; alternatively, use an all-over texture pattern
- Round cutter: ¾ in (20 mm)
- Knitting needle: size 7 (4–5 mm)

These sliding beads have a hole in the bottom edge from which you can hang charms from other sections of this book, allowing them to be incorporated into a bead charm bracelet or necklace. Converter beads are easy to make and can be decorated in various ways. Two different sizes are given here—the large bail is for pendants and the smaller bead is for bracelets.

LARGE SLIDING BAIL

1 Roll out a sheet of clay, 4 p.c. (1 mm) thick, and smear the surface with oil. Lay the clay, oiled side down, on the texture sheet and roll lightly over the back to take an impression. If it is not deep enough, ball up the clay, re-roll, and try again.

2 Lay the textured clay on a non-stick surface and cut out a circle with the round cutter. If the clay circle comes away with the cutter, push it out carefully with a finger to avoid spoiling the texture.

3 Place the circle, textured side down, onto a ceramic tile. Lay the knitting needle across the center. Brush the bottom of the circle with paste, then fold the top of the circle over the needle and press down lightly onto the bottom half.

4 Use a fine yarn needle to make a pilot hole in the lower edge of the bail. Dry the piece on the knitting needle. Remove the needle, sand any rough edges, and drill the hole with a 1 mm bit through both lower edges. Fire and polish.

CONVERTER BEADS

Antique look Oxidize the
sliding bail and then polish
back to accentuate the
impressed pattern.

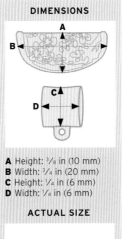

SMALL CONVERTER BEAD

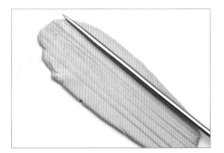

5 Roll out a sheet of clay, 4 p.c. (1 mm)
thick. Leave the clay plain or texture
with a pattern. Here, the side of a darning
needle is used to make parallel ridges in
the clay. Cut a ¼ x 1 in (6 x 25 mm) strip
from the textured sheet.

6 Lay the strip, textured side down, on
the work surface and place the knitting
needle at the top edge. Roll up the needle
in the strip until the leading edge of the
strip touches the clay below.

Texture pattern
Texture the clay with a
texture sheet or rubber
stamp before cutting out
the strip for the small
converter bead.

DIMENSIONS

A Height: ⅜ in (10 mm)
B Width: ¾ in (20 mm)
C Height: ¼ in (6 mm)
D Width: ¼ in (6 mm)

ACTUAL SIZE

7 Roll back a little and apply paste to the
point where the clay touches. Roll up
and press the edge of the strip onto the
paste to secure.

8 Cut the strip ⅛ in (3 mm) away from
the pasted join and trim to make a tag
of clay that hangs down below the sliding
bead. Make a pilot hole in the tag and dry.
Remove from the knitting needle, sand
the edges, drill the hole with a 1 mm bit,
and then fire.

Materials, tools, and techniques

Charms are traditionally very small pieces of jewelry, but they are so varied in shape and form that you will use many different techniques when making the projects in this book. This chapter gives you all the basic information you need for making charms with silver clay. More specialist techniques are given in the relevant projects.

MATERIALS, TOOLS, AND TECHNIQUES

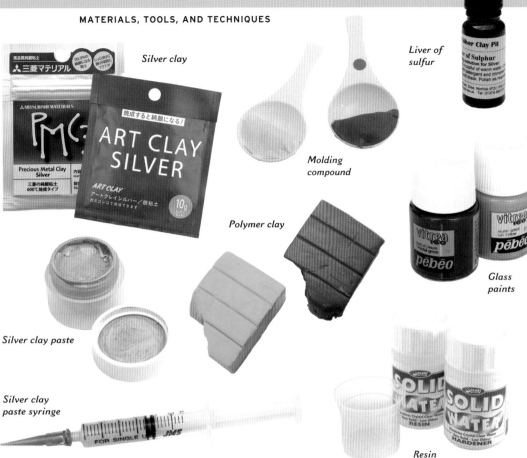

Silver clay

Liver of sulfur

Molding compound

Polymer clay

Glass paints

Silver clay paste

Silver clay paste syringe

Resin

Materials

Each charm project lists all of the materials you will need. The following are the main materials used. All are available from craft and metal clay suppliers.

Silver clay

There are two main brands of silver clay available: Art Clay Silver and Precious Metal Clay (PMC). The clay used in this book is fine silver clay that can be fired with a blowtorch or on a gas burner. Any Art Clay Silver clay can be used as well as PMC3. Other types can be used, but they normally need firing in a kiln; follow the manufacturer's instructions for firing.

Silver clay paste

Paste or slip is silver clay with added water that is used with soft and plaster-dry clay to join pieces together and make repairs. Ready-made paste is available but you can also make your own by adding water to soft clay. Paste or slip is also available in a syringe for piping and filigree effects.

Polymer clay

Polymer clay is a plastic modeling clay that is baked in the home oven to a permanent hardness. It is useful for practice sculpting, making molds, and embellishing silver clay. Follow the baking instructions on the packet.

Molding compound

Two-part putty silicone compound is used for making semi-flexible molds.

Coloring materials

■ **Liver of sulfur:** Available in lump or liquid form, this is used to oxidize the fired charms to antique them or add colored patinas.

■ **Resin:** Two-part clear coating resin is used to simulate enamel effects on metal clay. It is colored with resin pigments or oil paints. Resin that sets with ultraviolet light is also an option, but you will need a UV lightbox.

■ **Glass paints:** Designed for painting on glass, these paints are transparent, so the sheen of the silver shines through. The best paint to use for jewelry is the type that is baked onto the surface after drying, which gives a very durable result.

■ **Transparent inks:** These can be painted onto silver clay to add a transparent layer of color.

■ **Varnish:** A varnish suitable for use with metal is used to coat charms that have been oxidized or painted with glass paints or inks to protect the color during wear.

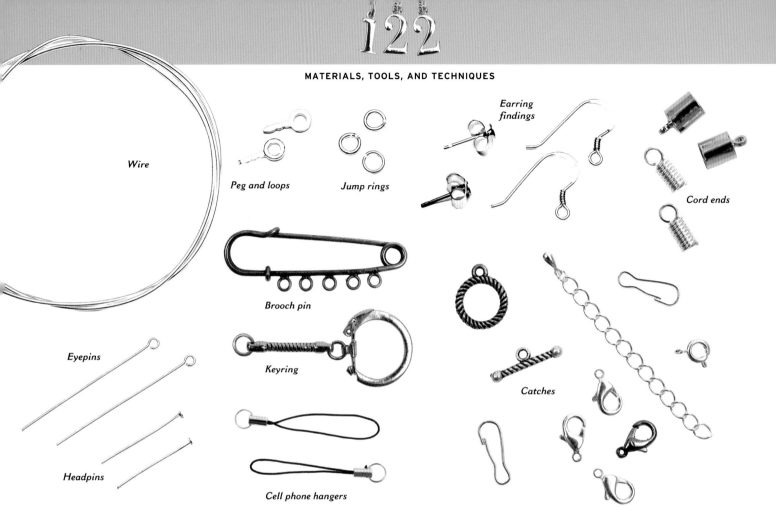

Wire

Peg and loops

Jump rings

Earring findings

Cord ends

Brooch pin

Eyepins

Keyring

Catches

Headpins

Cell phone hangers

Wire

■ **Pure silver:** Use this to make peg and loop findings for embedding into silver charms before firing. Only use pure silver because plated or sterling silver wire will break down when fired.

■ **Sterling silver:** Use this for jump rings and any other wire requirements after firing. It is stronger than pure silver wire.

■ **Silver plated:** This is an economical alternative to sterling silver. Colored wire is also widely available.

Note: Wire comes in different thicknesses. The most useful for charms are 24 gauge (0.5 mm) for small peg and loop findings and 20 gauge (0.8 mm) for most other purposes.

Chains and cords

■ **Chains:** These are available in all kinds of styles and thicknesses. Thick chain is used for bracelets, thinner chain for necklaces and dangle embellishments.

■ **Cords:** These can be used to make bracelets and necklaces. Materials include cotton, leather, rattail, linen, and hemp. They can be wound or braided.

Findings

These are the bits of metal used to create jewelry using charms. They are available as plated metal, sterling silver, and in finishes such as bronze or antiqued.

■ **Peg and loop findings:** Also known as screw eyes, these are embedded into charms as a hanging point. You can buy them or make your own (see page 131).

■ **Jump rings:** Small rings for attaching charms (see page 140 for how to make your own).

■ **Catches:** Closures for bracelets and necklaces or for attaching

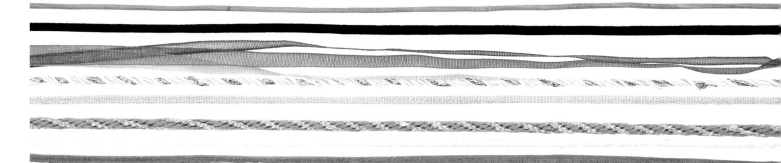

Cords

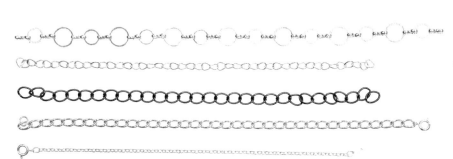

Chains

single charms. There are numerous types, including lobster clasps, toggle clasps, spring rings, and hooks.

■ **Cord ends:** For finishing the ends of cord bracelets.

■ **Headpins and eyepins:** Thread beads onto them to make dangles for embellishments.

■ **Earring findings:** These include fishhook earwires and flat pad studs.

■ **Other findings:** Cell phone hangers, keyrings, brooch pins.

Gemstones and beads

Use manmade gemstones that are guaranteed for firing into silver clay. Small glass beads can also be embedded before firing. Do not quench or the stone will shatter. All kinds of beads in glass, plastic, or ceramic and semiprecious stones can be used for dangles and other embellishments that do not require firing.

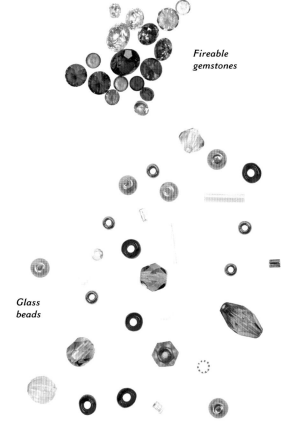

Fireable gemstones

Glass beads

Basic toolkit

The following tools are the essentials and, to avoid repetition, they are not listed individually for each project. Metal clay suppliers have all the basic tools for mail order, but kitchenware stores and cake-decorating suppliers will also have many useful tools.

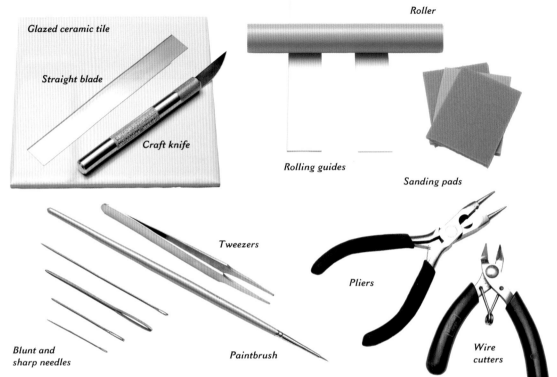

Glazed ceramic tile

Straight blade

Craft knife

Roller

Rolling guides

Sanding pads

Tweezers

Pliers

Blunt and sharp needles

Paintbrush

Wire cutters

Work surface

■ **Wipeable surface:** Work on a surface that can be wiped clean, such as a plastic or glass chopping board.

■ **Non-stick surface:** For rolling out thin sheets, use a piece of Teflon mat or improvise with a lightly textured plastic file pocket.

■ **Ceramic tiles:** These make excellent movable work surfaces and can be placed in an oven to dry the piece. Choose small tiles with a smooth, glazed surface.

Cutting tools

■ **Craft knife:** A curved blade is the most versatile; pointed blades are useful for detailed cutting.

■ **Straight blade:** Also called slicer or tissue blades, these are used for cutting straight edges and thin strips from sheets of clay.

Rolling tools

■ **Roller:** Plastic rollers for rolling out smooth, thin sheets of clay are available from metal clay suppliers or you can use a small glass bottle.

■ **Rolling guides:** These are strips of plastic that are laid on either side of the roller so that the sheet of clay is rolled out evenly to an exact thickness. Playing cards (referred to as p.c. in the projects) are a useful substitute. Stack the specified number of cards on each side of the clay.

■ **Log roller:** A sheet of clear Plexiglas or a CD case is used to roll neat even logs.

Needles

■ **Blunt yarn or tapestry needles:** These are used for sculpting and piercing. Large (size 13/2.25 mm) and fine (size 20/1 mm) needles are used in this book.

■ **Darning needle:** Long, sharp needle used for piercing.

■ **Fine sewing needle:** For cutting out around templates.

General tools

■ **Paintbrush:** A fine round artist's paintbrush, size 0 or 1, is used to apply paste and brush water onto the clay surface. Manmade bristles are best and durable.

■ **Pot of water:** You will need a small pot of water at all times for wetting the clay, washing your brush, and rehydrating the clay.

■ **Vegetable oil:** A light oil such as light olive oil or sunflower oil is used to prevent sticking.

■ **Plastic wrap and small jelly jar:** Wrap clay tightly in plastic wrap for storage. Small glass jelly jars are watertight and will keep wrapped clay soft for weeks.

■ **Tweezers:** These are used to manipulate delicate pieces of clay, add findings, and handle hot pieces after firing.

■ **Pliers and wire cutters:** For shaping and cutting wire. Fine round-nose pliers are used for turning loops and most other needs; chain-nose pliers are useful for opening and closing jump rings and for shaping wire.

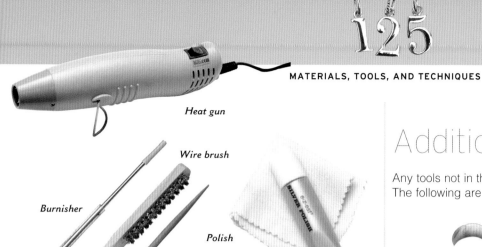

Heat gun

Wire brush

Burnisher

Polish

Drill bit and vise

Needle file

Additional tools

Any tools not in the basic toolkit are listed in full for each project. The following are used in several projects:

Cutters

Stamps

Metal tubes

Texture sheet

Ball tool

Tools for dried and fired clay

■ **Sanding materials:** Sponge-backed sanding pads come in different sizes of grit and the three finest are best for silver clay: superfine (the coarsest), ultrafine, and microfine. Cut into small squares for sanding charms. Sandpaper is useful for sanding flat surfaces on plaster-dry clay.

■ **Needle file:** A small fine half-round needle file will smooth irregularities in both plaster-dry and fired silver clay.

■ **Wire brush:** To brush over the surface of the silver after firing. Use a fine brush for details.

■ **Burnishing tools:** A fine burnishing tool is used to shine the silver surface. A large stainless steel yarn needle works as well.

■ **Drilling tools:** You will need a small (1 mm) drill bit for drilling neat holes in the charms for hanging. Clamp the drill bit in a pin vise for easier drilling.

■ **Polish:** Silver polish and polishing cloth or soft rag for polishing the finished charms.

Drying and firing tools

■ **Drying tools:** A home oven is a convenient method of drying silver clay. A hair drier is useful for quick surface drying; a crafter's heat gun is a hotter version.

■ **Firing tools:** All of the projects in this book can be fired using either a blowtorch and firebrick (see page 133) or a gas stovetop and stainless steel mesh (see page 134). Choose the method you prefer. You can use a small jewelry kiln to fire silver clay if you have one, provided that it has a digital controller to regulate the temperature (see page 134).

■ **Cutters:** These are available in lots of different shapes. Cake-decorating suppliers have small-scale cutters for tiny charms. Small round cutters are especially useful—use brass tube available from metal clay suppliers, model and hobby stores, and dollhouse supplies stores. Plastic paintbrush protectors or drinking straws can also be used.

■ **Stamps and texture sheets:** Finely detailed texture sheets and tiny peg stamps of $\frac{3}{8}$ in (10 mm) diameter are best for charms.

■ **Ball tool:** Used for sculpting and making indents. An $\frac{1}{8}$ in (3 mm) diameter ball is the most useful size. Improvise with a round glass-headed dressmaking pin.

■ **Hammer and block:** A lightweight DIY hammer and a small anvil or metal block are used to hammer wire to shape.

Working with silver clay

There are five main stages when working with silver clay.

1 Soft clay techniques: The first stage is to shape and model the soft clay. This varies from simple rolling out to more advanced techniques involving syringing clay.

2 Drying: When you have finished working the clay in the soft stage, the charm needs to be fully dried.

3 Pre-finishing: The dried clay (called plaster dry or greenware) can be further refined before firing. Dried clay is easier to work with than solid silver, but it is also more fragile.

4 Firing: This is where the alchemy happens, turning a piece of clay into solid silver.

5 Finishing: The fired silver charms are refined and polished, ready to wear.

Preparing the clay

Silver clay is normally in an ideal condition when first removed from the packet, but it is a good idea to knead it briefly. A small jelly jar is ideal for storing leftover clay and is more watertight than a plastic container.

1 Remove the clay from the package, including any that is stuck to the inner wrapper.

2 Knead the piece of clay briefly in your fingers to redistribute any moisture that has settled in the packet. It is now ready for use.

3 If the clay is too sticky to work easily when it comes out of the pack, roll it out inside a folded sheet of silicone baking parchment to absorb some of the moisture.

STORING CLAY
Tightly wrap any leftover clay in plastic food wrap and then place it in an airtight container. A small jelly jar is ideal.

Rehydrating clay

As you work, the clay will begin to dry out. Clay is too dry when it begins to crack or crumble as you shape it. Do not add water to the outside because this causes a slimy mess that is hard to control. The following method is the best way.

 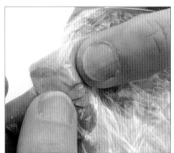

1 Roll out the clay as thinly as possible on a non-stick surface. This will crush any drying lumps in the clay. Spread a thin film of water over the surface of the clay and roll it up with the wet side inside.

2 Knead the clay thoroughly inside plastic wrap to contain the mess. Keep opening the wrap and folding the clay in half, then kneading again. Finally, remove the clay, and then roll out thinly and fold in half several times to complete the process. If necessary, repeat the whole process until the clay feels soft and pliable again.

Sculpted charms *Keep the clay well hydrated when sculpting charms such as teddy bears.*

Reconstituting clay

It is a simple process to recycle clay that has completely dried out.

Tools and materials

- Small cook's pestle and mortar
- Small strainer with fine nylon mesh
- Ceramic or glass bowl
- Eyedropper

1 Use a small pestle and mortar to grind up the dry lump of clay into a fine powder. For a really smooth clay, sieve the powder and regrind any lumps.

2 Add water a few drops at a time to the powder and mix to a stiff clay consistency. Knead in plastic wrap and leave for an hour, then roll out several times to complete the mixing process.

Shaping the clay

These simple shaping techniques—rolling sheets and logs, and forming balls and teardrops—are fundamental to working with metal clay and are used throughout the projects.

Simple shapes Charms such as steampunk turtles are made using simple shaping techniques: balls, teardrops, logs, and sheets.

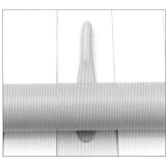

SHEETS
Flatten the clay into a pancake. Place rolling strips or playing cards of the required thickness on either side and roll with a roller.

BALLS AND TEARDROPS
1 Roll a ball of clay between the pads of your fingers, rotating the upper finger over the lower one until the ball is round and regular.

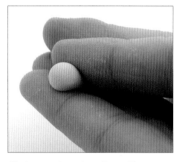

2 Form a teardrop by rolling one side of a ball of clay between your fingers to draw out a point.

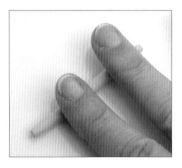

LOGS
1 Form the clay into a rough log and lay it on your work surface. Roll your fingers back and forth to lengthen it and thin the log.

2 To make the log even and thinner, use a log roller or piece of clear Plexiglas to roll the log further.

3 To make extremely thin threads of clay, hold one end of the rolled log in your non-working hand and use your other hand to roll the end of the log very lightly, pulling it out into a fine thread.

Molding

Molding works beautifully with silver clay. Molds for the charms in this book are made in polymer clay or putty silicone molding compound. You can make molds from existing pieces, or from pieces you have sculpted yourself in silver clay or polymer clay.

Syringing

This is a fabulous technique for adding detail to tiny pieces but it needs some dexterity. Try filling an empty syringe with toothpaste for practice with the different nozzles. The following shows the best way to hold the syringe for detailed syringing.

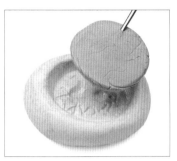

POLYMER CLAY MOLDS
Polymer clay is used to make fairly rigid molds of pieces that are quite shallow, such as coins or small sculpts. See Coins on page 34 for how to mold using polymer clay.

PUTTY SILICONE MOLDS
Putty silicone makes more flexible molds that can have slight undercuts and is used for more three-dimensional pieces such as shells. See Shells on page 40 for how to use putty silicone.

1 Hold the syringe in your working hand like a pencil. Use your other hand to press the plunger to extrude a line of clay paste. Dab down to anchor the beginning of a syringed line and then lift the syringe while pressing the plunger so that the line of clay falls into place as you move the syringe.

2 Dab down at the end of a line to cut the thread of clay.

JOINING CLAY PIECES
Many of the projects require pieces of silver clay to be joined together. Attach fresh pieces of clay with paste to make a strong join. Very thin pieces can be added by brushing the clay surface with water before pressing the fresh piece onto it.

3 You can make lines, curves, and dots using this method. Use a damp paintbrush to correct any errors or overruns.

Attachment holes

Some charms require a hole to be drilled as a hanging point. Make a pilot hole in the soft clay, and then drill through neatly after drying. You can drill the hole in a suitable place in the charm, or in a tag of clay added or left specially for the purpose. Use a clay tag for double-sided charms.

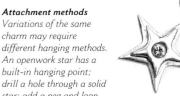

Built-in hanging hole
Some charms can be attached to jewelry and accessories by a jump ring or chain put through the charm itself, such as through the bow of the key charms.

DRILLING A HOLE

1 Pierce straight down into the clay with a fine yarn needle until it touches the surface below.

2 Dry the piece (see page 132) and then use a 1 mm drill bit held in a pin vise to drill the hole through neatly.

Attachment methods
Variations of the same charm may require different hanging methods. An openwork star has a built-in hanging point; drill a hole through a solid star; add a peg and loop finding to a gemstone star.

CLAY TAG

1 Place a small round cutter just over the straight edge of a sheet of clay at least ¹/₃₂ in (1 mm) thick. Cut out a D-shaped tag and paste the straight edge to the charm.

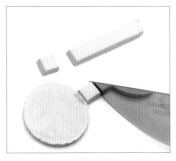

2 Alternatively, cut an ¹/₈ in (3 mm) square of clay. Brush paste on one side of the square and use a knife blade to push it against the charm. Trim the corners off to round them.

3 Use a fine yarn needle to make a pilot hole, dry the piece, and then sand the tag into a smooth curve. Drill the hole as described above.

MATERIALS, TOOLS, AND TECHNIQUES

Peg and loop findings

A peg and loop finding is the best attachment method for three-dimensional sculpted charms or those that require a delicate added hanging point. You can buy the finding or make your own using pure silver wire, which is then embedded in the silver clay before firing.

Tools and materials

- Pure silver wire: 24 gauge (0.5 mm) for tiny charms; 20 gauge (0.8 mm) for larger charms. Each peg and loop needs about $1/2$ in (13 mm) of wire, but it is easier to work from the wire coil
- Round-nose pliers
- Wire cutters
- Small hammer and flat surface for hammering on, such as a small anvil or metal block

1 Turn a loop in the end of the wire by gripping the very end with the tips of the pliers and turning the wire away from you into a complete circle.

2 Remove the pliers and insert them into the loop. Pull the loop back a little to center it on the length of wire.

3 Cut the wire about $1/8$–$5/32$ in (3–4 mm) from the loop. Hammer the resulting peg on your block to flatten it into a blade.

4 Insert the blade into the soft clay and use paste to fill any gaps around it. It needs to be held securely in the silver clay.

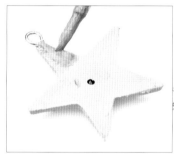

5 If the charm is not thick enough for the peg to be embedded, attach it to the surface with paste and cover the blade completely with more paste. After drying, sand into a smooth dome.

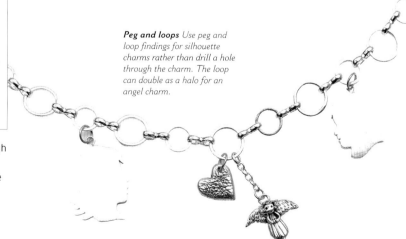

Peg and loops Use peg and loop findings for silhouette charms rather than drill a hole through the charm. The loop can double as a halo for an angel charm.

Drying

Silver clay must be fully dried before firing. Any water remaining in the clay will turn to steam during firing and cause cracks. Some charms also need to be partially dried as you work on them.

Pre-finishing

The dried clay can now be refined and smoothed before firing. Dried silver clay is called plaster dry or greenware and is relatively fragile, so take care. It can be sanded, carved, filed, drilled, and engraved, added to and pasted, or syringed with decorations.

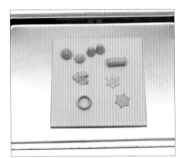

FULL DRYING
Leaving pieces to air dry in a warm place overnight is usually sufficient for tiny pieces like charms. You can also dry the pieces on a tile or metal baking sheet (not aluminum because it reacts with the clay) in a home oven set at 300°F (150°C) for 20 minutes (or check the clay manufacturer's recommendations).

PARTIAL DRYING
You can use a hair drier or hot air gun (used for embossing crafts) to dry charms as you work on them, after adding fresh clay or paste, but do not use this method for full drying. A hair drier can be used for several minutes at a time, but a heat gun should not be used for longer than 15-second bursts or it may burn off the binder in the clay.

SANDING
Use a superfine-grit sanding pad to sand away rough areas. Fill holes and cracks with paste, dry again, then sand once more.

FILING
Use a fine needle file to file into corners and curves to remove rough edges.

MENDING
1 If a charm breaks, use paste to join the two pieces together and then dry the piece again.

2 Sand the pasted join until smooth. The join will be invisible after firing.

Blowtorch firing

This is a fast and efficient method of firing silver clay charms after they have been dried. You will need a blowtorch and firebrick. Adjust the torch flame to a medium heat so that it is mainly blue but with a slight feathering of yellow at the tip.

Blowtorch *A simple handheld torch is inexpensive and ideal for firing charms. It is filled with butane gas that comes in aerosol cans.*

Firebrick *You will need a firebrick to fire the pieces on.*

CHOOSING A FIRING METHOD

Firing burns away the binder in the silver clay and heats the particles of silver to just below melting point so that they sinter into solid metal. Silver clay can be fired using a blowtorch, a gas stovetop, or a kiln. All of the projects in this book can be fired using either of the first two simple methods, provided that the clay you have used can be fired in these ways as recommended by the manufacturer. All types of Art Clay Silver and PMC3 are suitable. You can also use a kiln for firing if you have one (see page 134).

CLAY TYPE	BLOWTORCH FIRING TIME
Art Clay Silver (all kinds)	1 minute
PMC3	2 minutes
PMC+	At least 5 minutes

1 Place the dried piece on a firing brick. Aim the flame at the piece and after several seconds it will flare up into a flame, which is the binder burning away. When the flame has died down, the piece will begin to glow a pale orange.

2 Start timing from this point, keeping the piece at this orange color for the full firing time. If the piece starts to show a shiny silver surface, pull back the torch because it is melting the silver.

QUENCHING
Leave fired pieces to cool for 10 minutes or use tweezers to plunge them into a ceramic or glass bowl of cold water. Do not quench pieces that contain gemstones or beads or they may crack.

FIRING TEST
If you have not fired silver clay using a blowtorch or gas stove before, do a firing test to check your equipment. Roll out some clay, 4 p.c. (1 mm) thick, and cut out some $1/16$ x $1/2$ in (1.5 x 13 mm) strips. Fire the strips and then check that they will bend into a U-bend without breaking. If they break, your blowtorch or gas burner is not hot enough and you should fire hotter and for longer or use another method.

Gas stove firing

This simple firing method is easy to use. You can fire several charms at a time on the mesh. When the firing time is up, turn off the gas and leave the pieces to cool, or quench them (see page 133). If you have never used your gas stove for firing silver clay before, fire a test piece first (see box page 133).

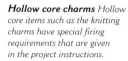

Hollow core charms *Hollow core items such as the knitting charms have special firing requirements that are given in the project instructions.*

Stainless steel mesh *You will need a stainless steel mesh, available from metal clay suppliers, for placing on the burner.*

Gas burner *A domestic gas stove or a camping gas stove are reliable methods for firing silver clay.*

KILN FIRING

All silver clay charms can be fired in a kiln on a kiln board. Refer to your kiln manual and the silver clay recommendations for firing times.

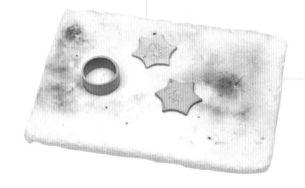

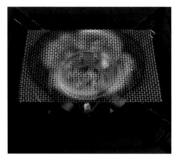

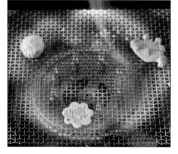

1 Place the mesh on the gas burner. Turn on the burner and note where the mesh glows red hot. Turn off the gas and place the dried silver pieces where the mesh glowed red.

2 Turn the burner on full flame. After a few moments the pieces will begin to give off small flames, which is the binder burning away. Continue firing until the pieces glow a pale orange, and then time the firing from this point.

CLAY TYPE	GAS STOVE FIRING TIME
Art Clay Silver (all kinds)	5 minutes
PMC3	10 minutes
PMC+	Not recommended

Finishing techniques

Once the pieces are fired and quenched or cooled, they are solid silver and ready to be finished. Freshly fired silver pieces have a white crystalline surface that should be brushed smooth. The result is a pleasing satin finish that can be left as it is or the charm can be polished further.

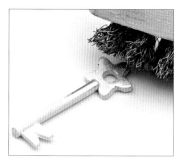

BRUSHING

1 Use a stainless steel dry brush or a soft brass brush and soapy water to brush the charm smooth and give it a satin finish.

2 Fine stainless steel brushes are available to get into the detail of small areas or you can use a fiberglass clutch pencil brush.

FILING

You can correct any details in solid silver with a fine needle file. Fine silver is quite soft and files easily.

BURNISHING

Use a stainless steel burnishing tool, or the side of a large yarn needle, to rub over the surface of the silver to burnish it to a shine. This is the best technique for small and textured pieces.

SANDING

Larger charms with smooth areas can be sanded to a mirror polish using three different grits of sanding sponges, working from superfine (the coarsest) to ultrafine and microfine.

POWER TOOLS

A hobby drill is a useful tool for polishing tiny charms. Use a set of silicone bristle disk brushes and work from coarse to fine to polish to a mirror shine.

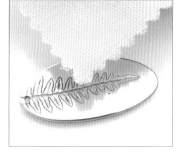

POLISHING

Use silver polish and a soft cloth to give a high shine to pieces that have been sanded or polished to a mirror finish.

Polishing charms
Take care not to break delicate pieces such as sails or remove detail from textured charms such as snowflakes.

Oxidizing

This technique is used to color the surface of the silver clay with rich patinas. A solution of liver of sulfur is used to achieve a range of colors, from pale gold to purples, blues, and black.

Tools and materials

- Liver of sulfur
- Cup of very hot (not boiling) water
- Dishwashing liquid or cotton swab and rubbing alcohol for degreasing
- Tweezers
- Varnish suitable for metal

1 Clean the polished silver charm with dishwashing liquid and rinse (or brush with alcohol). If the piece is not cleaned thoroughly, the patina will be patchy.

2 Add a few drops of liver of sulfur to a cup of very hot water. If you are using liver of sulfur in lump form, use a pea-sized piece.

3 Swirl the charm in the water using the tweezers. After a few moments, the piece will begin to color. The oxidation begins with a yellowing of the silver.

Color range The wonderful color range of liver of sulfur on silver clay.

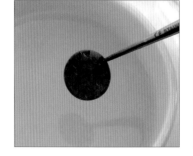

4 The colors usually progress through copper to purple, blue, and finally black. Rinse well when it reaches the desired color. Varnish over the piece to preserve the patina.

5 If you polish back, high areas will return to silver while the color will remain in the details. In this case, there is no need to varnish because the color will stay in the recessed areas.

Resin

Two-part clear coating resin is used to simulate enamel on metal clay and for embedding materials under a domed-lens effect. Clean the polished charm thoroughly with alcohol before applying resin. After application, leave the piece to set under an upside down glass tumbler for 24 hours or as required.

Glass paints

Glass paints add gorgeous translucent color to polished silver. Bakeable glass paints are the most durable.

Tools and materials

- Clear coating resin and hardener
- Coloring pigments or oil paints
- Mixing cup and spatula
- Large yarn needle for applying
- Cotton swab and rubbing alcohol for degreasing
- Glass tumbler

1 Mix up the resin according to the manufacturer's instructions (usually 2 parts resin to 1 part hardener or equal quantities).

2 To color the resin, add a match head of oil paint or pigment and stir well. Apply the resin in a thin coat with the needle, pushing it over the surface of the silver. Leave to set under a tumbler.

3 Uncolored resin can be domed over flat surfaces to make a lens effect for pictures, letters, and small beads. Always seal any embedded paper with varnish or decoupage medium before applying resin or it will discolor.

Brush the polished silver charm with alcohol to remove any grease from the surface so that the glass paint will adhere well. Brush the color generously onto the surface, then allow the paint to dry for 24 hours and bake as recommended to set the paint. For a more durable result, varnish over the color.

Tools and materials

- Bakeable glass paints in the colors of your choice (Vitrail 160 is water based and bakeable)
- Fine paintbrush and water pot
- Cotton swab and rubbing alcohol for degreasing
- Varnish suitable for metal

Ink colors Silver charms can also be painted with transparent inks to add a translucent layer of color. Degrease the surface first, and protect the color afterward with varnish. The delicate ink colors look good when alternated with plain silver charms.

Simple chain bracelet

There are many different types of chain available from jewelry-making suppliers that you can make up into your own bracelets. Clasps also come in a wonderful array of shapes and sizes or you can even make your own in silver clay.

AVERAGE BRACELET LENGTHS (INCLUDING CLASP)	
Young child (3–5 years)	5 in (12.5 cm)
Child (5–12 years)	6–7 in (15–18 cm)
Teen	7–7½ in (18–19 cm)
Adult	7–8 in (18–20 cm)
Adult plus	8–9 in (20–23 cm)
Custom size	Wrist circumference plus 1–1½ in (25–40 mm)

Tools and materials

- Chain in the metal and weight of your choice
- Clasp: a lobster clasp and large jump ring are used here
- Jump rings of a suitable size for the charms and link size of the bracelet
- Pliers and wire cutters
- Masking tape or sticky tape

1 Measure the length of chain required, allowing for the length of the chosen clasp. Cut the length of chain by cutting through a link with wire cutters or by pulling a link apart with pliers.

2 Attach the clasp to one end of the bracelet using a jump ring (see page 140). Attach the large jump ring to the other end.

3 Tape the bracelet down on a work surface, leaving a bit of slack so that you can lift it. This prevents the bracelet from twisting as you work.

4 Lay out the charms along the bracelet. One-sided charms should be attached to the bottom of the chain links so that they hang down and show their fronts. Double-sided and 3-D charms can be added more randomly.

5 Open a jump ring and, holding it in your pliers, thread on a charm, facing upward. Lift the chain a little and loop the jump ring through the link. Close the jump ring and then repeat to attach the other charms.

Braided cord bracelet

Braided cord bracelets in silk, linen, leather, or cotton are very popular and can be made in many different colors.

Multicolored cord
Braiding three different colors makes a design feature of the cord, but you can use a single color if you prefer.

1 Clip one end of the three cords to the top of the ruler with the binder clip. You can rest the other end of the ruler against your body to keep it steady while you braid.

2 Work down the cords, passing each outside cord over the center one alternately until you reach the end.

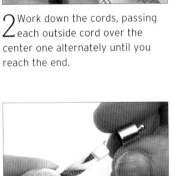

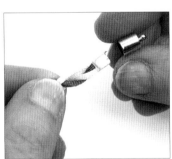

3 Trim the end to neaten, then smear glue over the end of the cords and bind tightly with a small strip of masking tape. Remove from the clip and cut the other end to length. Bind in the same way.

4 Smear more glue over the masking tape binding and glue each end inside a cord end, making sure that the tape is concealed inside and trimming the end if necessary.

5 Allow to dry and then attach the clasp to the loops on the cord ends. Attach charms to the individual cords of the braid with jump rings.

Tools and materials

- Cord in the colors and thickness of your choice: three 9 in (23 cm) strands of 2 mm satin rattail cord are used here
- Cord end findings wide enough for the three strands: use a 4 mm internal measurement for three 2 mm cords
- Binder clip
- Ruler
- E6000 glue or strong PVA glue
- Masking tape
- Clasp: a toggle clasp is used here

Jump rings and chain links

Jump rings are the small rings used to attach charms to bracelets, necklaces, and other types of jewelry and accessories. They can be purchased but it is easy, and more economical, to make your own. The same technique can be used to make links for a chain bracelet.

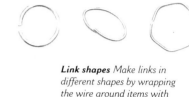

Link shapes *Make links in different shapes by wrapping the wire around items with different cross sections.*

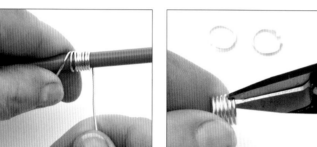

MAKING JUMP RINGS

1 Wind the wire tightly around the knitting needle or dowel about ten times; each turn will be a single jump ring.

2 Slide the wire coil off the knitting needle and cut through each ring with the wire cutters, one ring at a time.

USING JUMP RINGS

Using two pairs of pliers, open and close the jump ring by pushing one end away from you and pulling the other end toward you. Do not pull the ends away from each other to open or the ring will distort.

Tools and materials

- Sterling silver or silver-plated wire: 22 gauge (0.6 mm) wire for small charms; 20 gauge (0.8 mm) for larger charms
- Knitting needle or piece of wooden dowel: $1/8-5/32$ in (3-4 mm) thick for small charms; $3/16$ in (5 mm) or larger for bigger charms
- Wire cutters and pliers

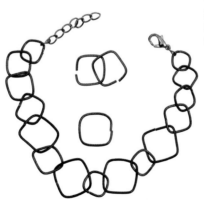

HANDMADE CHAIN LINKS

Try making large links for a bracelet by winding colored wire around a thick pen or piece of dowel. Cut the links as for jump rings, then assemble by connecting the separate links. Add a clasp.

WIRE JIG

Use a wire jig, available from jewelry-making suppliers, to make interesting links to join into a link bracelet with matching jump rings.

MATERIALS, TOOLS, AND TECHNIQUES

Embellishments

Use dangles and beads to add color and interest to charm bracelets and other jewelry. They look pretty hung singly or in groups between charms.

Tools and materials

- Sterling silver or silver-plated headpins: 1 in (25 mm) long
- Selection of small beads, rocailles, seed beads, etc.
- Round-nose pliers and wire cutters
- Jump rings

BEAD DANGLES

1 Thread beads onto a headpin. Larger beads at the bottom add balance.

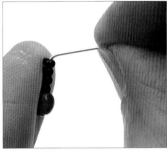

2 When you are happy with the arrangement and number, pull the protruding end of the headpin over at a right angle just beyond the last bead. Trim to ¼ in (6 mm) from the top bead.

3 Using round-nose pliers, turn a loop on the end of the headpin (see page 131). Make sure that the loop is centered over the top of the headpin.

Tools and materials

- Sterling silver or silver-plated wire: 0.8 mm (20 gauge)
- Lightweight DIY hammer and small anvil or metal block
- Knitting needle or crochet hook
- Wire cutters

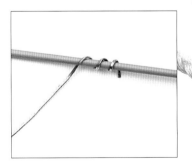

WIRE DANGLES

Flatten a length of wire by beating it with a hammer on a metal block. Wrap it around a knitting needle at an angle, then cut into lengths and form a closed loop at the top of each dangle.

Double dangles Attach dangles to a chain or cord with a jump ring, grouping or spacing them between charms. Two dangles on a jump ring give a richer effect.

Index

Credits

We would like to thank the following companies for supplying materials for this book:

For supplying PMC3 silver clay:
The PMC Studio UK
Weylands Court
Watermeadow
Chesham
Buckinghamshire HP5 1LF
Tel: 01494 774428
www.thepmcstudio.com

For supply Art Clay Silver:
MetalClay Ltd, UK
27 West Street
Corfe Castle BH20 5HA
Tel: 01929 481541
www.metalclay.co.uk

For supplying silver bracelets:
Kristian Wimshurst
Diss Antiques
2/3 Market Place
Diss
Norfolk IP22 4JT
Tel: 01379 642213
www.dissantiques.com

For supplying silver page numbers:

Azendi
31 Otley Road
Leeds
West Yorkshire LS6 3AA
Tel: 00 44 (0) 113 278 9919
www.azendi.com
email: customerservices@azendi.com

All images are the copyright of Quarto Publishing plc. While every effort has been made to credit contributors, Quarto would like to apologize should there have been any omissions or errors—and would be pleased to make the appropriate correction for future editions of the book.

Further resources
Silver clay and all of the tools and materials required to make the charms in this book are widely available from metal clay suppliers and art and craft stores worldwide and by mail order from online suppliers. Sue Heaser's website—www.sueheaser.com—has further information on the tools and materials used in her books. For detailed information on working with metal clays, see *Metal Clay for Jewelry Makers: The Complete Technique Guide* by Sue Heaser.